THE LADY & THE HARE

WITHDRAWN

PAULINE STAINER

The Lady & the Hare

NEW & SELECTED POEMS

BLOODAXE BOOKS

ISBN: 1 85224 632 4

First published 2003 by
Bloodaxe Books Ltd,
Highgreen,
Tarset,
Northumberland NE48 1RP.

Second impression 2005.

www.bloodaxebooks.com
For further information about Bloodaxe titles
please visit our website or write to
the above address for a catalogue.

Bloodaxe Books Ltd acknowledges
the financial assistance of
Arts Council England, North East.

Cover printing by J. Thomson Colour Printers Ltd, Glasgow.

Printed in Great Britain by
Bell & Bain Limited, Glasgow, Scotland.

In memory of Giselle

ACKNOWLEDGEMENTS

This book draws on Pauline Stainer's five Bloodaxe collections, *The Honeycomb* (1989), *Sighting the Slave Ship* (1992), *The Ice-Pilot Speaks* (1994), *The Wound-dresser's Dream* (1996) and *Parable Island* (1999), and also includes a whole collection of new poems, *A Litany of High Waters* (2003).

Acknowledgements are due to the editors of the following publications in which some of the new poems first appeared: *Aireings, The Bridport Anthology 2001, Leviathan Quarterly, Near East Review, Oxford Today, Poetry Ireland, Poetry Review, The Rialto* and *The Times Literary Supplement*. 'The Reversible Waterfall' was commissioned by Poems for the Waiting Room. The title-sequence of *A Litany of High Waters* was commissioned and published by the King's Lynn Poetry Festival, 2002.

CONTENTS

FROM **The Ice-Pilot Speaks** (1994)

FROM **The Wound-dresser's Dream** (1996)

FROM **Parable Island** (1999)

A Litany of High Waters (2003)

THE HONEYCOMB

(1989)

The Honeycomb

They had made love early in the high bed,
Not knowing the honeycomb stretched
Between lath and plaster of the outer wall.

For a century
The bees had wintered there,
Prisoning sugar in the virgin wax.

At times of transition,
Spring and autumn,
Their vibration swelled the room.

Laying his hand against the plaster
In the May sunrise,
He felt the faint frequency of their arousal,

Nor winters later, burning the beeswax candle,
Could he forget his tremulous first loving
Into the humming dawn.

The Figurehead

He came upon her strangely,
Whilst driving through night-mist:
A ship's figurehead under apple trees
Where the village forked.

The slant-moon
Touched her breasts with spindrift,
Bleached hair
Swept back from her brow;

Her nakedness
So eerily illumined in the orchard,
He saw nothing,
Driving till dawn,

But her beached body,
And through her eyes
With their unchiselled pupils,
The bitter cresses blowing in ghost-ports.

Figures in a Landscape

You can see landscape through their eyes –
The wide, green-folded dreams
Of king and queen.

Swallows cleave their bronze cheek-bones;
Crowned they are
With field-garlic, fool's parsley.

She bears the silver-torque of the snail's trail;
The moon plumps out her breasts
Like sleepy pears.

He, with a hole in the thorax,
Wears floating sedge over floating-rib,
Cresses in the heart's alcove.

If they speak,
It is with hart's tongue:
With fern, self-seeded invisibly on the wind.

Inlaid they are;
Their limbs lichened
As with immortal lesions.

They survive all dissolving mediums.
But at stubble-burning,
Through vanishing points of smoke,

They raise for a moment
Earthly bodies to unearthly light,
Lovers in an assayer's fire,

Whilst at their feet
Red clover blows
As if they bleed.

The Airfield Falcons

There are larks here now –
where once falcons
flew the airfield
from the wrist.

Their enforced hunger,
their whistling-down
to the gauntlet,
taint the wind.

You can sense it still:
the lure of flesh,
the bloodhawk
at the green plover;

the war-machine timed
to tear out
the red timepiece
of the heart;

and down the vanishing runways,
a subtler knell –
the flashing abstract
of the kill.

The Bowls Match

Being short-sighted,
she had trusted
the opthalmic surgeon
to refocus light with the knife;
cut close
to the visual axis,
alter the curvature of the cornea
with a diamond-tipped scalpel.

Looking up,
she saw the sun through the glass,
and beyond the hospital hedge
ladies on the lawn
playing bowls
in crisp hats and light summer clothes,
hands raised above their heads
to clap a victory.

Their applause
for unerring alignment
was silent through the pane;
and they should have worn
changeable silks
for her perfected vision –

but she saw them
as if from a clerestory,
stout and middle-aged
in the undeceiving distance,
arms upheld in hierarchy,
radiant figures
at the scene
of an unidentified miracle.

The Gargoyles

As she climbed the cathedral tower,
One of the canon's daughters
Was married in the choir.

She looked down on the maze;
The bride wore
Waxen blossom in her hair.

She passed the door to the belfry;
'In tissue of silver
And cloth of gold' sang the choir.

She came out on the flashing.
It is the lead on the nave roof
Shines so silver.

Gazing down,
She saw the reception
In the bishop's rose garden,

Minute tables under damask;
through the O of the water-spouts
She glimpsed the wine waiters;

And they, glancing up in the late sun,
Caught the scream of gargoyles
Before she leapt.

Walking the Water

Feet skirr the membrane –
the child before birth
walking the water.

Siphon from the sac;
amniosis
is ghost on a glass slide.

X-ray the running light;
the lit watermark
of the flesh.

Divine
the foetal heartbeat,
the pulse through the caul.

Corpuscles are cautionary magic;
crucifixion
a red suspension in the blood;

visitation
a velvet-runner –
the spirit sexed.

The Catalyst

Long after the birth,
she held up the x-ray
of her second-born son
in the womb.

There he hung
against the light,
head-down to the lintel,
translucent
as wax in a glass.

What she saw
was not simply
the curve of the spine,
the seal at the cervix,

but sacrament brightly stilled;
an angelical stone
that cannot be weighed;

the catalyst
of sun through wax –
the ghostly body –
at the casual supper
Christ eating the honeycomb.

The Ballad of the Lock-keeper's Daughter

'Why do you sit by the window,
With cheek pressed to the glass?'
Make up the fire, mother;
My baby sleeps so fast.

'I hear the hiss of skates
In the thin March dusk.'
It's the wind in the thorn, mother,
By the green lock-gates.

'The skating-party are out
On the frozen reach.'
Lock the door quickly, mother,
There's blood-spoor over the ice.

'They are bearing a silver fish
Out of the thinning mist.'
Pull down the blind, mother,
Whilst the skaters go past.

'Or is it a milk-white hound
Caught in the sluice?'
Turn the lamp high, mother;
Heart's blood is a fugitive dye.

'It's a shape of the beaten-silver,
In a shawl pinned fast.'
The milk stands proud on my breasts, mother;
But my baby, sleeps at last.

The Misericord

Turning up the misericord,
He found the girl, the unicorn couched in her lap,
Her arms ringed round the white belly.

The O of her arms enfolded him, cool as vellum.
Looking up, he glimpsed the virginal boys,
Chill children in candlelight;

White boys of differing height,
Blanched under surplice;
He saw the falling intervals of their beauty –

And was circled a moment,
Like the unicorn in her arms,
By their bloodless brilliancy.

The Drawing

He outlined the bones
On the boy's body
With a fibre-tip pen.

The biology class crowded round,
Copied the pattern of scapula,
Femur and humerus.

The boy's body was fine-boned,
Like a slender hound,
With an ivory pulse at the throat.

As he ringed the breast-bone,
The rib-cage shimmered
Through the skin.

Had he flayed the flesh,
The bright lattice
Could not have shone more sheerly.

Fear rose
That he would stammer out
The luminous beauty of the soul's white cage.

Looking up, he saw his shaking hand,
The boys' suspicious gaze;
And grief struck him –

Not how they would misconstrue his trembling,
But that the soul's tremor in a boy's body
He could not draw.

The Plaster Room

Do not be deceived
By the hushed complexion of the room,
By the snow-moulded limbs.

Blanched disciplines abide here;
Medieval scissors hang on the wall,
Cages and casts, scrapers and cutters.

Patients filter in from the fracture clinic;
Green-stick children, supple as willow,
Their pliancy stilled under pallor.

Compound fractures from casualty,
The muted landscape of x-rays
Clipped to their stretchers.

The dying, with de-calcified bones,
The lace of their bodies
Beyond bone-setting.

The plasterer sluices his milky hands
Under the tap;
Caresses their effigies, like slip-ware –

With pure manipulation,
Sets a seal on their suffering
As in absolution.

Ballad of the Abbot's Fishpond

By the abbot's fishpond
Brother Gilbert has run wild,
For he has found a drowned girl
And she with child.

Flowers he gathered for Our Lady –
Saw the carp
So stilly-green
Browsing on her body.

Throughout the abbot's sermon
He had smelled the meadowsweet,
As if Blodeuwedd's beauty
Were conjured at his feet.

They have brought him
To the chancel,
They have rung
The sacring-bell;

There is linen on the chalice
White as the unborn lamb;
Wafers in the paten
Finer than vellum.

He does not hear; he cannot speak;
Sees nothing during Mass,
But how the sun illumined
Her breasts beneath the glass.

For by the abbot's fishpond
Brother Gilbert he ran wild:
He found Our Lady's body
And she with child.

The Elderbrides

It was the day
She first noticed
Her breasts growing.

She sat on the summer-house step;
Felt them tilt
Through her slip.

They shook
Under the cambric,
White does in shade.

It was then
She smelled the elderflower;
The gypsy-blooms,

The rank-dreamers
Who shake out shawls
For the dead.

They trembled above her head,
Five-petalled, five-stamened,
Vibrant in the breeze,

And suffused her body,
Fleeting, equivocal,
In bridal with the stealing sun.

The Blood Spoor

I followed the blood-spoor
Into upland border-country,
Where the doe drops her fawn
Below the snow-line,
And carrion crows
Wait in cloud-shadow
For the afterbirth.

I crossed the glazed gully;
Here the hart,
Driven from the etched coppice,
Had once crouched
In the running stream
To keep his scent
From the hunt.

Going higher,
I reached the barrow,
Its site almost ploughed out;
But still the spoor
On the fresh-turned furrow –

As if the Saxon princes
Had cast their clay-quilt,
And turned subliminal faces
To the rubric,
The red-stitching;

Remembering the high horns
In the hounded blood.

The Coffin

*(A boy was found buried between two hives
at Marathon in Ancient Greece.)*

They have buried a boy
between two hives
placed mouth to mouth;

housed him
horizontally
in the baked-clay;

a cemetery
of faint fragrance
under fragments of brace-comb.

The bees
encapsulate those dead
they cannot bear away,

seal crevices
with resin
to exclude the light,

immure
the larval flesh
for imago –

Is that why
they cradled him so,
mouth to clay-mouth,

recalling the liquefaction
of the swarm above the hive
before flight

when one angle declines,
another is lifted,
the radiant mantle
into four sunlit corners?

[Maeterlinck, *The Life of the Bee*]

The Divining of Wounds

O Mary, woe for his lying down
The priest cuts in the wax a cross;
we must put out the wounds by burning.

The body is a pierced vessel,
the flesh beeswax;
O Mary woe.for his lying down

We divine from wounds
the stress of transcendence:
we must put out the wounds by burning.

Wounds draw: who are those
ranged round the anatomy theatre?
O Mary!, woe for his lying down

The burning at Hiroshima
raised their arms like rushlights;
we must put out the wounds by burning.

Strike fire –
light a candle for the hallows.
O Mary, woe for his lying down
we must put out the wounds by burning.

The repeated line is taken from Lewis Glyn Cothi's
On the Death of his Son, translated from the Welsh
(Gwyn Williams, *The Burning Tree*).

Flora in Calix-light
(after David Jones)

It was as if
you had cut the light
with a blade
of alchemical temper –
the bright-trailing briar,
the rippled chalice,
the brimming of brilliancy.

I was unprepared
for the haunting of radiance;
but did not the Saxon king
in the ship-burial
suffer ten silver bowls
chased with crosses
at his shoulder?

In the cool gallery
I glimpsed cup and corn,
necklace and calix,
the flower and the seal:
inspiritings
on a glass ground,
electric composure.

Calipers cannot measure
the drawing-power
of the wound;
the percussion
of crystal and water,
the sensuous atonement
of the light.

Nor is there any specification
for miracle:
for ungirdling the sun
against the day of burial.
But years later,
I saw the priests
walking on Armageddon

and remembered
the deep nectaries,
the dynamics of mercy,
caritas
the blood-red petal
against bewilderment.

Raking the Japanese Garden

What would Leonardo
have made of it –
the flowing gravel,
the raked spiral,
the unbroken wave against stone?

Here in the monastic garden,
expertise is the zoning
of desire;
enlightenment
the craft of the vanishing-point.

Particulars perfect the ground:
the tilt of rock,
shifting-centre of pebbles,
red lichen an accidental oxide
in the glaze.

In this fugal landscape,
holy conversation
is between circles that never touch,
luminosities
of perilous edge.

Nothing else has ever been
the scarlet persimmons
over the wall,
the parabolas
of their particle chamber,
will not recur.

Intuition is the blade
of the swept vision;
in the overnight snow
the samurai
rinse their swords.

Marksman

You must draw the bow
against the blade of the light;
measure sprung-release
by thrown shadow
on a sheer backdrop.

Coldly intemperate
are the angles of incidence
into the heart –
even the samurai's breastplate
laced with silk –

the mastery of recoil
to look up at the unidentified figures
on the battlement
as if *no tremor*
runs through the body.

The Flute Lesson

Today in history of art
we did Roman wall-painting,
studied a frieze of musicians
from Herculaneum;

fluteplayers –
their mouthpieces
still fresh-whittled
from under the hot lava –
master and pupil
fingering the stops.

What caught in my throat
was not their swift embedding,
but how at that last lesson
before my parents knew,
you took the flute from my lips
pressed your mouth to mine
and flutter-tongued.

The Dancing Mistress

It was the first time
I had seen her
with her glasses off –

usually she was backstage
at the dancing-school's annual matinee,
a martinet standing over the box
where we rubbed our points
in the rosin;

but I had left the other girls,
run along the concrete corridor
silently in my ballet pumps –

and there she was,
embracing my friend's father
in the deserted cloakroom,
pressed between the iron pegs
above the mesh lockers –
he with her glasses in his hand.

What I remember
is not so much their unguarded anger,
or the feeling I had sped
unsolicited from the wings,
but that glimpse
of some other

less accountable order.

The Boating Party

They saw blood in the woods
but the body was never found
It might have been Les Sablonnières:
the ambush in the mist,
autumn crossfire,
an undivulged wound.

La fête étrange
in No Man's Land;
rime on his battledress
beside the bridlepath;
in the small meadows
water racing beneath the ice.

Ascension Thursday he first saw her –
glimpsed her again
at the December boating party
on the shifting marsh,
her hands ungloved a moment
on the gunwale.

But still she walks
whitely to Mass
on Whitsunday –
closes the shutters
against the high wind in the spinney
before her winter wedding;

while he, from no known grave,
bears her uncoffined body
down the narrow stair.

Alain-Fournier was killed on the Western Front; his grave is unknown.
The opening lines are from *Le Grand Meaulnes.*

The Birth

The hypnotist laid her in trance.
'You are seven,' he said,
'Sing the songs you remember.'

The surgeons bent over,
Masked above the mound of her belly,
Made the incision.

She sang of green rushes.
They severed the membranes
Releasing birth-waters.

'You are turning the school rope.
You are singing to skipping
In the sunlit yard.'

O make my love a coffin
Of the gold that shines yellow;
They swabbed the bright blood.

Her voice rose over the cord:
The wind, the wind, the wind blows high
She'll die for want of the golden city.

They held the child up,
Dark-freckled like a fritillary;
Its cry pierced her singing.

Snake Handler

They sway in the snake-pit,
serpent and handler,
hermetic dancers.

Wizard and hooded king,
white-bellies wreathed behind glass,
holy ones.

Mesmerised children
flatten their faces
against the cobra's kiss –

and for a moment
the venom hangs on the glaze
like a seraph.

The Dream of Pilate's Wife

Last night
I saw the moon
dark with the great cavities
of the body

I sent the soldier
to tell him
how I suffered
such a dream.

I saw you half-naked
shown to the people,
and I in an upper room
under fair linen.

Suddenly in the sun,
the crowd was burnished away
by your body for burying –
the magisterial wounds –

and I in the upper room
under fair linen.

Cargo

We found beeswax on the shore
as we beachcombed
that summer;
threw the misshapen lumps
into the burning driftwood;
let them flare
into the sea-wind.

We knew of no wreck
for so strange a cargo;
but dream still
of the black wax
in the bleached wood,
the visitation of salt,
the resinous haze.

How faint the fuel –
the drift
of the dreaming gene –
the precipitation of dead
bearing on their clavicles
bee-necklaces of amber.

The Crossing

There was no alert
that winter:
the great cats came quite calmly
from their cages
across the frozen moat
into the public enclosure;

no sound
except the slight pressure
of sinew on snow,
no deeper solstice
than the hinge
of their jaws;

and if we saw them
a moment
at a remove –
the curving warmth of a bird
between us
and their weight on the ice –

it was only like glimpsing
the thaw in a mirror –
recognition made strange –
that crossing
illusory, ruthless,
when the pursuit of quarry

unleashes the dream.

Stepping Off the Aqueduct

Easy to step off the aqueduct –

far below
the cricketers stream
from their pavilion
onto the cunning green;

nothing but the stone-lip
of the canal
between narrow-boat
and the sheep drowsing
under the hawthorn.

Even now, in still afternoons,
I sense that passage by water
above the running-weirs of the river –

the slung shadow of the towpath,
the weightless clarity,
the slight freight of the heart.

FROM

SIGHTING THE SLAVE SHIP

(1992)

Sighting the Slave Ship

We came to unexpected latitudes –
sighted the slave ship
during divine service
on deck.

In earlier dog-days
we had made landfall
between forests of sandalwood,
taken on salt, falcons and sulphur.

What haunted us later
was not the cool dispensing
of sacrament
in the burnished doldrums

but something more exotic –
that sense
of a slight shift of cargo
while becalmed.

Piranesi's Fever

It could have been malaria –
the ricochet of the pulse
along his outflung arm,
grappling-irons
at each cautery-point on the body.

She lay with him between bouts;
pressed to his temple
the lazy estuary of her wrist;
brought him myrrh
on a burning salver.

How lucid they made him,
the specifics against fever:
the magnified footfall of the physician,
the application of cupping-glasses
above the echoing stairwell,

windlass and shaft,
the apparatus of imaginary prisons;
a catwalk slung across the vault
for those who will never take
the drawbridge to the hanging-garden.

None of this he could tell her –
that those he glimpsed
rigging the scaffold
were not fresco-painters,
but inquisitors giddy from blood-letting;

that when he clung to her
it wasn't delirium
but a fleeting humour of the eye –
unspecified torture,
death as an exact science.

Only after each crisis, could he speak
of the sudden lit elision
as she threw back the shutters
and he felt the weight of sunlight
on her unseen breasts.

A Haze Held by Thorns

A jeweller's wheel cuts the constellations
above the circular garden
on the single canvas

the white doe folds her feet into tallowed alabaster;
the dancers pour their shawls
like glazes over the balustrade

beside the seven immaculate triangles of water,
the dead wear their trembler-springs
of hammered gold

the sun notches its arrow;
the pomegranate bleeds;
the virgin wears an ermine on her sleeve

the timbre of the light
a haze held by thorns,
a snakeskin still perfect over the eye.

How it burns back – the myrrh at noon –
the milk from the crushed nectaries
of her breasts –

and beyond the palings,
where the paired birds hang
on their frieze

the falconers
walk into the crucifixion.

The Blue Beret
(after Rembrandt)

In the *Raising of the Cross*
you painted yourself
in a blue beret
assisting at the crucifixion.

Is death
so fixed a tincture
none at the atrocity
escape recognition?

Soft –
even now
in the *Descent by Torchlight*
you help him down,

wearing neither beret
nor doublet,
but bodies
interlaced

for flesh
is the outlandish dress
at the recurring
deposition.

To Saskia, with Pearls in Her Hair
(after Rembrandt)

Four pregnancies
and only one surviving son –
I sketched your dishevelled sheets
for the *Death of the Virgin*.

Painting your last portrait,
I remembered how I had drawn you
in silverpoint
three days after our betrothal;

how for an early etching
you wore a fillet of warm pearls,
and when I made
the first pure pull from the plate

I saw your breast
through the split bodice
whiter than
the shaft of a quill.

The Red King's Dream
(for Graham Arnold)

It is one of those white stone days;
the Reverend Charles Dodgson
is in his darkroom
developing on large glass plates
the exposures
of a girl's body.

I look through the key-hole
into the Deanery garden,
sisters on the croquet lawn,
the air full of hedgehogs
up, down, strange, charmed
like quarks

my queen scowls
at the topiary
a quickset hog shot up
into a porcupine,
a lavender pig with sage
growing in its belly

gauzes drop from the fly-tower;
the Furies are for real,
endgame an axe –
the alchemist
dressed in tinsel
hanged with a yellow rope

but time runs slower
nearer the earth;
the oars are feathered,
the executioner
pelted with roses,
and from a skep

on the White Knight's saddle,
bees swarm into
the scented rushes
where a girl holds
mirror-writing
to the river.

Angel-roof

They rise on bleached wings
from the pure maths
of the hammerbeams;
more frugal than El Greco's angels
who drop one wing
as if grace were mettlesome.

What startles
is not how they blanch the dusk;
but the tilted roof-mirror
which magnifies their wounds
for their breasts
are peppered with shot;

and outside, untouched by such candour,
disparate fuses burn;
sheep graze the salt-marsh,
and brushing the transepts,
the faint rank hawthorn
races the blood.

Structuring the Silence

This is the landscape
of the Old Masters:
a single figure fishing
below the precipice,
the floating sleeve
of the mist.

Our horses hesitate
before the steel hawser
across the bridleway,
the pungency
of riffled sawdust,
the felled tree.

We date the core
in failing light;
see where the outer rings
flow together as if
to assimilate the sun,
gaze at the stain of impact;

remember the red-earth
calligraphy
freely painted
under the glaze
of the Chinese pillow
for the dead

and having abstracted
the oracle-bones from silence,
felled stillness
at a stroke –
we sway slightly
like spirits balancing in the saddle

and ride on.

Transparencies in a Landscape

Speedskaters *en grisaille*
streaking the fen
like trace over smoked paper

a heron on the ice,
fish suspended
into steel-engraving

deer grazing
the moon from the leaves:
the moment at gaze.

Time is dense with such inclusions –
vesicles in the rock,
crystals that grow in the body

the luminous inconsequence of
the sign which suffices;
adze and ripple

of riverlight
through the split
where the arrow is notched

our lips wet
with the brief dew that falls
during eclipse.

Music for Invasive Surgery

Hush is unnecessary.
Surgeons operate on the ear
to the sound of string quartets.

Hands make division on a ground:
moving parts are revealed
like a skeleton clock.

Why is excision
the most haunting
of disciplines –

the divining of affliction
never appropriate –
the music to which the unicorn kneels

death and the maiden?

The Ringing Chamber

I was four months gone –
my breasts already tender
against the bell-ropes;

we were ringing quarter-peals,
the sun flooding the bell-chamber,
the dust rippling between the joists

when the child quickened,
fluttered against the changes;
and suddenly through the clerestory

I saw that colder quickening –
random, reciprocal –
cloudshadow

and the flaxfield
like water under the wind.

Skydivers

They fall outwards
as if from the calyx of a flower
each smaller than a falcon's claw,
their target a gravel circle
in the Byzantine barley.

They fall like hushed flame
where once the sun's disk
was ploughed from the furrow,
coupling, uncoupling
above the drop-zone.

When they run
with the white squall
you would think the air
holds their flight
like a welder's seam,

but as they alight
there's a sudden
billow of pollen,
an uprush
from winged heels

and like lovers,
the sweet tarrying
of their bodies
dissolves
the moment.

The Falconer's Bride

Before the hawking party
you stroked the falcon's breast
with a little switch;

showed me the immature plumage,
transparent hunger-traces on the welts,
the shafts still full of blood.

It was a skill you said
to keep a hawk from sleeping,
marry its speed with the wind.

I have embroidered lure and hood with noble metals;
cut from supple leather
the sliding-jesses worn even in flight.

You gave me the white gyrfalcon in Lent;
but today, I remembered
how you filled your mouth with water,

sprayed it through closed lips
onto the restive bird's breast –
and her sudden pure mantling.

The Yew Walk

What is the distance
between us, you said
when we slept naked
but barely touched;
the quilt thrown back,
streaks of moth-dust
across your breast.

That night I dreamt
you brushed against
the trees of the yew-walk;
the strange fine pollen dust
shook out,
sifted most eerily
inside your dress.

I do not know
why its green-gold
so long unloosed
kindled your nakedness –
or why I woke to kiss
the estranging dust
the single flesh.

The Victorian Head Dress

I dreamt I had to find it
for my second wedding,
with its seed-pearls
and lilies
on their silvered wire.

The whole light summer night
I searched;
wondered why we furnish the dead
when the living wear
such stiff flowers.

The wedding-car came,
the solstice whitened
over the salt-marsh,
refracted wading-birds
knelt in the silt

but how coldly it flared –
the wax in my hair;
and through the windscreen
the glass-cage
of the sun.

The Reprieve

If I did not see them at first
it was because
they were skating on sunlight,
the shin-bones of animals
shaped to fit
under their shoes.

I never knew
whether it was pollen in the wind
or refracted sun from the saltings
which gave them
the cunning tooling
of haloes.

You said later
you had missed them;
but I saw you
among the cloud of witnesses –
unaccountably silenced
by the kiss of their blades.

Leonardo draws Bernardo Bandini

(hanged for the murder of Giuliano de Medici)

You noted the costume
as if compiling an inventory:
tan-coloured cap,
doublet of black serge,
dark hose;
red-stippled velvet
at the swinging neck.

How cool a faculty,
when you bequeathed
no silver instruments of surgery,
but drew
soft against stopped heart,
a blue coat lined
with fur of foxes' breasts.

A Party of Musicians in a Boat

No inventory mentions them –
though precious pigments
are noted:
two florins for ultramarine.

What is their pedigree –
those who beguiled
the Madonna of the Little Masters
with divisions on a ground?

Little is needed
to improvise against melancholy:
hour-glass and dividers,
a composition of figures.

Did they play for Leonardo
who strung the silver-skull,
when lakes were shoaled
with hibernating swallows?

Mysterious are those
painted to music;
but what of these
raising the burnished spinnaker?

Will the wind take their sails?
Even at the Annunciation
the sand runs
through the hour-glass.

How is it
they withhold
so hauntingly
the timing of departure –

shrouds
bright against the light,
the blood-red drummer
beating the silent bar?

Enclosed Wheatfield with Rising Sun

(this painting by Van Gogh once belonged to Robert Oppenheimer)

It is high summer.
I see the wheatfield
from the cell of my asylum;
when the wind blows from the south-east
I remember how the Romans
boiled saffron in the amphitheatre at Arles
to counteract the reek of blood.

I slept there in the yellow house
under a blood-red quilt;
the colours hissed
like metal in a mould;
I even flayed a frog,
held it to the great light of the Midi
for the intravenous lilt of the blood.

Some would have painted the sun
purple-black as a plum,
a fireball in the mouth
of a corpse;
or like Pentecostal flame,
dragonsblood,
one glaze bleeding into another.

I whipped it
until it cartwheeled like a sunflower
red on yellow
splashing the wheatfield
scarlet, pale sulphur,
a falcon
with a flail over its shoulder.

But last night I dreamt
of irradiating
all the colours at once –
as if the sun climbed
both sides of the canvas –
and in the silence
before the blaze

the high white note
of birds igniting
in mid-air.

Watersnake

How blackly
he wore the water,
rearing his saffron head
above the brackish cistern.

We had walked up
from the ruinous amphitheatre,
the olives birdless
in the salt wind;

it defined their shiver –
the way his liquid amber
left virtually no wake
in the sun –

but like Tiresias
before the divining draught,
he held silence
in his mouth

and it gushed again –
the oracle in the bloodstream,
the dead articulate
without their wits.

Source

Stone-masons from the monastery
work deeper and deeper
in the quarry,
always striking water
from the stone.

Meltwater roars
in the throat of the pumps,
the subsoil black
as with artesian
bleeding.

When the water runs clear
over the red rock
you hardly know
which fount
they tap

for the glancing play
between rule and source:
pure flux –
the reciprocating-pump
of the heart –

and when the sun
quickens the wellspring
that seminal bound –
the spilt-blue
of the virgin.

Christk to Charon

You probed my palms
with a boat-hook
as if they were runes
from a border-country.

'You a mercenary then?'
you asked
as we grounded
mid-stream.

You began
to navigate by echo:
wondered what depth of wound
you had plumbed.

But leaning
over the gunwale
you saw the rising dead
in the blood-wake

'Must mercy
be seen to bleed?'
'Compassion kills'
I said.

Goslar Warrior

(after Henry Moore)

The Greeks too are calm:
a man hurling a discus
will be caught
at the moment in which
he gathers his strength

Not for you –
you have caught
him off balance,
the tilt of the shield
against the falling warrior;

on the spinning battlefield
the ancestors
are unslaked,
their impetus
iron in the artery;

and you, the sculptor –
why should you feel
that weight in the heartwall
to control the reel
from the blade

when for a moment
the air is gifted
most terribly
with his blood
pumping?

Fire-bringers

the air darkens
with winter swallows
in the red-light district
of Bangkok

as they drop to roost
the tattooist needles
a vivid bird
just over the breast

O sister swallow
hectic
between magnetic fields –
such flicker

and below
streetwise girls,
lovers tonguing
the vulva

Togare

I have trained tigers
to spring at deflected light
from a dagger.

Take us on long exposure –
man and beast
ribboned with topaz like duellists.

They flinch at a flash,
brindled under the arc-lamps,
paws quilting the sawdust;

no inadvertent wound
except the sprung-release
of children

following me from the ringside
with the perishable inlay
of their eyes.

If suspended on a thread
and struck
that blade would sound

indefinitely

Mrs John Dowland

Do they ask after me
the foreign musicians,
when you play the galliard
for two upon one lute?

Cantus high on the fingerboard,
Bassus on the lower frets;
hands changing position
above the rose?

Here there is no perfect measure
for the visitation of the plague –
no resolution
for figures on a ground –

only the memory of how
you brooded over my body;
and the speaking harmony
with which, beyond all music

I would stop your lips.

Glass-men

Tonight
beyond the glow of charcoal
the gondolas leave
bluish-opal trails,
the sea-mist spiced with woodsmoke,
grids of chestnuts roasting

when the boy beckons
between the braziers
I remember the bodies
of glass-blowers, half-naked
against the furnace –
hot gathers of glass at the end
of each iron

how when they put
their salt mouths
to the blowing-rods
molten, manipulative,
I felt the lagoon rise
in the tidal dungeons.

St Sebastian

His body is juiced sweeter
than any girl's,
his tormentors
snooded in the wind.

It tilts at silence –
the way quicks
of whitethorn
lodge in his vitals

the technique of martyrdom
shafting, sexual,
a cicatrice
misterioso

How should we read
such carnal knowledge
as the wounds
whistle by?

Woman Holding a Balance
(after Vermeer)

We x-ray the embryo;
tap the womb
for the sex of the unborn;
but are haunted
by your composure.

Inclining your cool head,
you weigh
what we have found
questionable:
woman as diviner.

It could be gold-dust
in the scale-pans;
graded pearls;
or freight of souls
for the Last Judgement.

But the balance is empty;
and you keep
the equipoise
of anonymity
with downcast lids.

We cannot weigh
the serenity of genes;
measure purity by mirrors;
but when you
suspend the scales

You embody
such stillness,
we could believe
light from your high window
incarnates a child.

Speedskaters

They streak down
the water-grid
sexless between
the swelling sallows

bent forward
without feature
as if they have
jettisoned caprice

muscle and blade
in bloodless rhythm,
only deadline
seaming the silver.

But as they graze
the hazels,
the sudden
soft-focus lens –

pollen flurried
above the red stigma –
the steeled timing,
the rare confusion.

Stag

What was the metalled edge
along which I drove
when he sprang
from dark to dark

his head
escutcheoned
against the spinney
in the undipped lights?

Not black-ice,
the wheels locked
in skid –
but an older elision –

skeletons in
foetal position,
one of a child
cradling antlers.

Equipping the Spirit

They have made a hole
below the pyramid
with a carbide-tipped drill,
lowered the camera
onto libation tables
of blue granite.

It startles –
the physicality of afterlife –
the dead pulling flax
with gilded nails,
seven celestial cows
reclining

the sacred eye
restored to its socket,
each mummy flanked
by vertical snakes
with oblong hearts,
the sons of Horus
levitating above the lotus;

but is the heart weighed
with or without blood?
For in the nesting coffins
the sky-goddess
straddles the king
and the sun roars
between the lions of the horizon.

Hardy supervises the removal of graves
for a railway cutting

Even as apprentice,
the unswerving vision –
coffins along the iron road,
flare-lamps
whitening at dawn
under St Pancras,
and to the lit edge
of each bright pit,
their pelts irradiate with drizzle,
lowland foxes, lightly running.

Brunel Springs the Bridge

They drew me across
as I was dying.
I lay on my back,
heard the rumble of the open wagon,
watched the girders thresh overhead.

How busy the air was
at this altitude;
burnished insects
dropped past me
mating;

the stress
above the estuary
not pier and cantilever,
but gossamer
snagged on my waistcoat,

those random things
which had burned
there always,
invisible
as noon-tapers.

Modern Angels
Eight poems after Eric Ravilious

(In 1942, Eric Ravilious was sent as a war-artist to Iceland. On September 2nd, the aircraft in which he was a passenger, failed to return.)

1 *The Exercise*

You glimpsed it once –
the perfect hieroglyph
of a young pilot plunging
on training session into the dark sea
when *the exercise had to go on.*

Always you'd painted bright displacement:
the unquiet radiance of empty rooms,
a brazen ship's screw
on a wagon in snowscape,
the odd angle of those sleeping in the fuselage.

Lastly, sketchbook in hand,
you left on a patrol from Iceland,
never knowing how that exercise too –
the war-artist on active service –
ruthless, shining, would go on.

2 *Spitfires on a Bright Runway*

They stand in their rippled reflection
exact
but for mysterious digits;

their sprung-release
held glistening under watercolour –
as if the painter knew

beyond, on the ancient fen,
a breached dyke
has flooded the deer-park
and the deer wade
into the swollen waters
jostling, glittering

against the sun.

3 *Sussex Quarry at Night*

Here, where the chalk figures
flow with the downs,
you watched engines whiten
under arc-light and flare
with fine powder from the quarry;

men as magicians
at the exposed chalk wall,
exotic particles
settling in the hot slipstream
as in a winter garden;

each step a white flaw underfoot;
hedges shrouded
as if to deaden vibration;
no stranger palimpsest
till later

from the train window
you saw the body of the wheat
lean with the wind,
and turf-cutters scour
the white horse beyond

to purest bone.

4 *Hares Manoeuvring*

'And the following day we asked the whole searchlight
party in to eat large hares...' ERIC RAVILIOUS

In peacetime
we would catch them in our undipped lights
on the old airfield,
their spoor swerving down the frosted runway,
their gaze red.

Hypnotic
such searchlight on the retina –
each skull whittled
by darkness
to the blazing nerve;

a riving Cowper knew,
opening his little hatch
in the still square at Olney
to watch the hares gambol
against the heightening dusk

their eyes rubied,
their grey necessity
to out-manoeuvre madness –
for only after deliberate play
did the quiet quicken.

5 *Magnetic Minefield*

You had always
used light coolly
as if moving glass gaming-pieces;

found the most dangerous work
at low-tide
salving mines from the oyster-beds;

so it came luminously,
the posting to Iceland –
ivory seascape in relief

danger made pure.

6 *De-icing aircraft under the midnight sun*

This is the blue hour
which pigment and palette
will kindle and dispossess;

pillars of red light
to stimulate the heart;
the swung-lamp of the sun

illumining water-worn ammonites
in the glacier,
bluish, luminous,

and beyond,
more terrible than ice,
radials blading the wingspan

propellers of spun-blood.

7 *The Sealskin Gloves*

It was your first
and only letter from Iceland;
you asked if I would like
a pair of sealskin gloves –
What size shall I buy, you said.

None of the wariness
of a last self-portrait,
face almost erased –
Draw round your hand you said
a week after your death.

We glimpse it still –
the spatial mystery of the machine –
a broken water-turbine
in a stream;
wrecked harriers
beached like modern angels
on strange shores;

pleasure-steamers
ghosting the night
in their winter quarters;
the speaking-tubes
on the bridge of the destroyer
springing like African lily
under shelling at sea;

infernal engines
on a bright slipway –
and from the flightdeck,
with all the inconsequence
of revelation,
the crossing arcs
of afterburn.

FROM

THE ICE-PILOT SPEAKS

(1994)

The Ice-Pilot Speaks

I

No such thing
as a routine death –
in *ultima thule*
the shaman stretches
the throat of a walrus
over his drum.

It is Ascension week;
the men wear black crêpe veils
against snowblindness,
the ship's astronomer
is given four ounces
of raven;

sterna paradisaea
is caught with ordinary cotton;
a number of snowy owls
are shot,
one thawing its prey
against its breast.

O terra incognita –
the tundra is silk-crewel work;
polar-bears sweat
through upturned paws,
the ship's figurehead
warm as from the furnace

the sagas redden –
on tinted lantern slides
Amundsen drives
five of his dogs
to death
Language, open the sacred quarry.

II

I dream of your body
when there is no open water
and the Inuit women
soften foxskins
with their teeth.

It was like drawing
without looking
at the paper
as I ran my hand
between your breasts

but you remembered the nuns
at the silk farm
blanching the cocoons,
teasing out
the single thread

raw silk running

III

i

Like Quakers
the icebergs recline
their nudes

the light from their viscera
so blue, addicts can
no longer find the vein.

ii

Gymnopédies
Satie seeking
the antique whiteness

the estuary
swinging its mirrors
at right-angles

a looking-glass quadrille,
pistons counselling
perfection.

iii

Disquieting muses –
subtext
of the deep keels

the bisque-doll
on the seabed
mouthing the Titanic.

IV

Is it minimalist –
the music
for a northern light

fleece growing along
a sheep's spine, lava slowing
under high pressure hoses

the ship's surgeon cutting flesh
from between the ribs of the dead
to feed the living?

What is the sound
for such interstices –
the Piper Alpha wailing

fenders on the Silver-Pit
blistering at
the golden scenario

those two divers on the spiderdeck
underwater
at the time of explosion?

V

The high scree makes one dream –
ptarmigan hunters
use the snow as reflector
where they roost unseen,
the eight Inuit mummies,
one with Down's syndrome.

The blood-group of mummies
can be determined;
so what is this slippage
when you put them up darkly,
the white dead
already meditating flight

and the hunters are silenced
not by the muzzle-flash
from a gun
but by that sense
of encounter
with their own coffin?

   VI

What is song
when the shroud
is left unlaced at the mouth
and the arctic tern
has a radio transmitter
lashed with fuse-wire
to its leg?

What are footings?
Reindeer kneel
to the cull;
in Eller Moss
was found the skeleton
of a stag
standing upon its feet

At the magician's house
I carve ivory noseplugs
in the shape of a bird
with inlaid eyes.
What is the spirit
at gaze

the deerness of deer?

VII

St Brendan's monks
sail through the eye
of the iceberg.

At first, they ran
with the shadow of the land
through light bluish fog

later, by moonlight,
the ship caulked
with tallow, shamans

clashing over the Pole
as if to earth
any dead in the rigging,

and at dawn,
floes gliding by,
chesspieces in lenten veils

the sea a silver-stained
histology slide,
the O of the iceberg

whistling like Chinese birds
with porcelain whistles
on their feet.

Even in prayer
they could never replay it –
the purity of that zero

Varèse, playing
the density of his flute's
own platinum

the intervening angel
bearing a consignment
of freshwater.

VIII

Pestilencia!

The living wear
the black death
like windroses,
red for the quarter,
green for the half-winds.

Who says plague
is monotonous?
Christ turns
on Yggdrasill
under the strobe lights

I am my beloved's
his desire is toward me
and the dead stiffen
under their many eiders.

IX

In the North West Passage
William Newton, ice-mate,
hallucinates:

under the mosquito net
Marguerite
braids her hair

We sleep apart
as if we were dead

but o the searching
tongue of the sea

each time the muslin
billows the bed

a leopard coughs
in the camphor tree.

X

Up she rises –
the sunken softwood ship
with her dissolving
cargo of sugar,
fainter than
the eight hooves
of Sleipnir
on the albumen print
of the glacier.

Pittura metafisica
the mistletoe shafting
Balder; Borges
feeling the pillar
in his hotel room
at Reykjavik,
the Euclid of childhood
flowing through him
like serum.

One waterfall is extraordinarily like another
but for lovers
who kneel at its lip
and drink from
an unspilled moon
the source is altered
utterly,
until the painter,
erasing their figures

draws five strings
down the canvas
and hears from behind
the golden mean
the rasp of the salt-lick
as on the evening
of the first day
a man's hair
comes out of the ice.

XI

Sfumato!

The blue whales are flensed
by steam winch;
local reds
boil from the heart.

The whalers could be
gods, butchering
Balder's horse against
the midnight sun.

Loki is bound
with his own entrails
but who will wear
this smoking scarlet?

XII

We are close-hauled;
the narwhals hang
belly to belly
in the water.

I run my finger
through your menstrual blood
and put it to my mouth –
O Sigurd, who understood

the speech of birds
and slit the mailshirt
grown into her flesh
as Sigrdrifa slept

not a drop runs over,
but there is no room for another
and outside
the warm ice rafting.

XIII

They had no faint object camera –
whether they saw pack-ice or fog-bank
or mirage, will never be known

the weather not quite reliable,
leprosy
that white list in the sky.

So what made our love-making
the palimpsest
for all successive acts

when in the sedge-meadow
the gods are discovered
at chess

and give over
on their marvellous boards
the game that must be lost?

The Lady and the Hare

They would have you believe
she slept on bedrock
where ash roots the stone

that what startled silence
was not a buzzard mewing
but the huntsman's horn unblown.

When the hounds
broke from their thicket
they froze at her calm

sensed in the cold apse
of her breast
both the dove and the bone.

Today we started no hare;
downstream of the waterfall
found only her shrine

and how sternly
the warm hare is folded
inside her fierce gown.

Pointing Lady in a Landscape

(after Leonardo)

How can we read her simply
as she ghosts past
so entirely *rubato*
that water would wear
her impression
like an oculist's seal?

Is it the physiology
of the smile,
printed on silk
so thin
the image can be seen
from both sides

or the sleight
of quantum movement,
the verve
of her barely being there,
the fate of all those lost
probabilities

when given half a chance
she would swallow
the pearl of the moon?

Frequencies

I *Kettle's Yard*
(for Jacqueline du Pré who played there)

Then came the courtier Death
saw how she held the cello
in embrace like a lover,
and remission
the fleet accomplice,
the harmonic pitched with bravura;

beyond
a rippling-stitch of light
over fen water –
white willow
cut in white bud
stripped with the sap rising.

II *Frequencies*

The burning-glass
swings in the sun,
rings under vibrato;

in the dry valley
musicians gather to find the sound
to which the stones intone;

below foxholes
the great frieze floats
across the calcite crystal –

the ammonite,
coldest of grave-jewels,
clear quartz where its body was;

such intrinsic music –
the pliancy of the lens,
the implosion of the geode –

we do not know
whether their answering intensities
are wounds or wide roses.

III *Mirror-Canon*

There is some kind of exchange always
tapestries flow like plainsong
in the cleansing river

light plays on the still-life with dice;
a window embrasure is refracted
through the halo of the Christchild

passing-soft the note between harmonies
love as a bundle of myrrh between the breasts –
passing-soft the note between harmonies

through the halo of the Christchild
a window embrasure is refracted;
light plays on the still-life with dice

in the cleansing river
tapestries flow like plainsong
There is some kind of exchange always

IV *Prism in a White Room*

i

For you,
I would take out
the prism in a white room

the oblique kindling
from buried Pharaohs,
a crystal inserted to lighten the face

Turner's late white canvases
of nothing, and very like
horizon lost in absolute calm

the arctic hare's tibia
notched like a gnomen
into calendar of the moon

trace-element from metalpoint,
a thin silver stylus
for the end of time.

ii

Anguish not gravity
flaws the crystal –
morphine frozen in the syringe

at the sheer threshold
of avalanche –
white steppe-foxes

stunned by
blunt arrowheads of bone,
their pelts undamaged.

iii

Mystery is mute;
the cores of ancient snow
burn and atomise;

with heavy dust-like bloom
the quince hang golden
into the frost.

V *Aôroi*

The Greeks had a word for it:
those whose death is untimely;
before the concert
the young cello-player
wears gloves against the chill.

It is not music
that disarms,
but notation
of fern-staves
through the breast-cage.

The dead are contemporary;
their instruments
still strung with their hair,
their leaping chords
still dividing the pulse.

We must comb for amber;
keep time
in order to lose it;
ecstasy
our grave estrangement.

Between Stations

Between stations
not anywhere in particular
you put your neck on the line;
the train was delayed
above the water-meadows;
an ordinary suicide said the guard.

For a moment no one spoke.
Looking out,
I walked the weir-gate after snow;
saw the young swans
dip to the meltwater
below the roar of the foam.

And I have remembered
the marvellous interlacing
of their throats
against an unspilled reach
not anywhere in particular
but between stations.

Sarcophagus

Today
in that cold yellow pause
before the rape fluoresces,
I saw the blue glow
of plutonium

men in masks and boiler-suits
on the roof
of the sarcophagus
running, running
with divining-rods in their hands

nimble as matadors,
the sun catching
the sellotape at their ankles,
the speech of birds
graphite against the sky

the oracular dove
nesting
in the reactor.

Xochiquetzal

The firefighters of Chernobyl
lie naked
on sloping beds
in sterile rooms,
without eyelashes
or salivary glands

o death
take them lightly
as the Colombian goddess
who makes love
to young warriors
on the battlefield

holding a butterfly
between her lips.

The Dice Players

The painter has arranged them
around four light sources
as if the spilling of dice
were logical

the lutenist playing
lilac negatives,
the moment selected
for its obliquity

and outside the frame,
objects in melancholy
relation; dusk;
velvet revolution

an outbreak of cholera
at the masked ball,
lovers exchanging tongues
like matchless birds.

Christ in a Chimerical Landscape

Do the resurrected remember
the lilt in the blood,
the donor heart
of the red practitioner
who reduces bodies
to perfection

the meld
of pheromones
as Christ and the Magdalen
intinct the bread
and the yellow lilies lie down
with the snow-white lion?

Do they hear
the mercuric music
thin as cat-ice
as the bones vibrate
along the sightlines
of the serpent's skull

the wild bees
hanging like mistletoe
from the transom
before swarming
into the hole
in Christ's side?

The fountain
sways its root
when from the extracted body
bruises migrate
like birds
and the gardener

made her all greene
on the suddaine.

Burying the Green Boy

Japanese physicists gather
to study the crop rings;
they measure humidity,
electro-magnetism,
hoping for the occasional double centre;

they try so hard
with their ball lightning
apparatus,
simulating circles
in a plasma chamber

but the Green Boy
reaped the static here once,
where the round barrows
hold their foetal dead
like *chakras*

and they will not catch
the circle as it forms –
stalks whistling
with the moist wind
of the Apocrypha –

any more than they will catch
the edge of that moment
when he steps
from the intense spin
of the barley

slips a metal sleeve
on the whetstone.

Lot's Wife

She still asks
questions about rain
in the wind
from the Dead Sea

the oryx drawn
to her salt-lick,
the myrrh tree
oxidising

her handprint
redder than
blood-orange
against the rock.

But above her
on the thermals –
what concentrates
the lens

into the hawk's eye,
as she turns
on her axis
of crystallisation

calcium surging
through her cells,
the dry-brush stroke
over her orifices

seamless
as moonrise?

Thaw

Why should meltwater
press so
on a wound?

The bodies of Victorian climbers
are recovered
as the glaciers retreat

erratics
in the malachite green,
backlit by the sun.

It can still open an artery –
that glimpse
of their release –

uncorrupted, roped-together
as if death
were a minor master.

Axe
(after Michelangelo)

They have put the pietà
behind glass
because a lunatic
lopped-off the Madonna's hands.

I replay each stroke
in slow motion
as if the five principal wounds
were not enough.

She looks too young
to be his mother,
but at the swish
of the axe

the punishing red
on the white relief
floats the word
Take. Eat.

and she takes him
like a lover
on her tongue
back into her body.

Magtelt's Song

The sixteen virgins
come down from the gallows
to the *music of chance*,
cinnamon and cassia
falling from their yellow hair,
the sizzle of snow
in the holes
where their hearts once were.

Ah sister flesh,
when their hearts came out
and clouded the steel,
the wound sang the knife
until under the ice
a crystalline stone
rang in the inner ear
of the fish.

Oxnead Hall, Norfolk

Byrd composed here –
the dead rise
through the underair
on their sugarlift etching;

in the still-room
rose petals are drying
for the wedding
of the daughter of the house;

windows open simultaneously –
polyphony,
the sudden alembics
distilling Corpus Christi

and the bridegroom
who will play her body
without looking
at the music.

Paragliding over the Spice Routes

It's as if the blood billows
over the parachute-shadow
on the sea

azure sensation
of gossamer-harness
along the skin

white terns diving,
the moving ruffle of shoals
just under the surface

an indigo upsurge
as the wind freshens
to the smoking horizon

and beyond the curving wake
of the speedboat
tensile, shining

vessels drawing their cargoes
into the haze
more whitely than adamant.

This Atomising of Things

In the dustless
centre of the lake
artisans sieve powdered
gold into lacquer

differing meshes,
spangled ground,
not so much fusion
as the smoke from it

ashore – beasts
of soft red sandstone
smouldering
along the spirit road

and the after-touch
of a girl warming
a pouch of silkworm eggs
between her breasts.

Lepers at Dunwich

Distance is different here –
between dissolvings –
dust fine as pouncing rosin
under the fresco
where the angels have lost their sandals

do not look at the lepers
but the spaces between –
the phrasing of spray
against sandstone,
martins mining the undercliff

attrition is
iodine on the wind,
the hairline eroded,
no purchase for the compass-point
to swing its halo

immunity
to ravish the unlovely –
even without lips
they are brides
of Christ

and he holds them
indissoluble
in the salt undertow
as if after the first drowning
there were no other.

Threshold

I

Everywhere
the luminous inconsequence
of little interiors

Gwen John waking
to the unseen colours
of flowers culled at night

St Francis
preaching to the birds,
the quantum leap

of the stigmata
eight minutes ago
in the sun

the swan entering Leda
like laser
through alabaster.

What precipitates bliss
when nothing
is arranged

not even the sabre
in the frozen air?

II

He was flayed alive
after sacrilege –
his skin still under
one of the church hinges

the bees build
in his bone lesions
between the keyhole
and the later masonry

I detect
as by ultra-violet
their wax tabernacles
his viscera

that earlier torture –
the ribs broken
until his lungs winged
each side of the spine

even now at night
they give off
phosphorescence,
small fragrance

and beyond,
electrified vortices
of red and white
over the crop rings.

A Blind Man Passes La Sagrada Familia

I

I have no spittle on my lids

I hear the light quadrupeds
squirrel, ferret
on the seven lesser altars

the sough of birds
chloroformed
with outstretched wings

still-born infants
rising on plaster dust
in the Santa Cruz hospital

the triple torchères
tossing their howling manes
for the three holy children.

II

I feel the flexible wire-mesh
of the recording angel
on the Field of the Harp

skeletons
practising deposition
from pulleys and weights

doves of polished iron
in the spandrel
as if heaven were to one side

the billow of incense
through the twelve bell-towers
each blowing a different death.

III

I sense the cranes rust
along their rat-lines, men like trees
walking the spiderdeck

the hare kindle
at the annunciation
in the bloody meadow

Lazarus
densify the ice-house
under the lawn

the desire to crucify
by mirrors, calvary flowing
until it floats

the pestles of the mortars.

IV

I see the masons
chip the stone
into blazing accidentals

the spires cast
their Venetian glass like falcons
into the wind

the seraph
at the empty sepulchre
in a suit of lights.

Bird in Space

It is not a bird,
it is the meaning of flight
the pale curve
to the underwing
earthed by the rainbow

the swivel and leash
of Egyptian falcons
slipped from a mummy's fist,
their night pricked
as for transfer

the flare
of honeywax birds
set alight
by the mass-candles
at which they sipped

the perfect pitch
of harriers
through stained-glass
browsing
from calvary

the quantum physics
of swifts
as they descend
footless
into the pentagonal garden.

Quanta

I

Reality happens
when you look at it –
the deer fawn
in the vertical light,
the crystal hunter
is killed by a single falling stone
on Annapurna.

But what perfects the casual –
Vermeer buried with three children
of unspecified sex,
the shaman in the glacier,
a crystalline disc pressed
to the strange blue tattoos
still intact on his breast?

II

*Things happen
simultaneously
and in every direction
at once*

hail drives
through the samphire
where the ammonites
show signs of healing

high-level
radioactive waste
is turned into molten glass
sealed in stainless steel

a pyx of white silver
is laid in a silken
compartment
in Christ's body

the limbs of mummies
crackle like chemical
glass-tubing
and give out great heat

the ovens work continuously;
no part of the prisoner is wasted;
dental gold is returned
to the Reichsbank

the city swings like a cradle –
the seven vials
spill their seven plagues
into the rubble

up above somewhere a fox crosses over
and the daughter of Jairus
is raised behind the geranium
on the windowsill.

III

What is for real
is the marvellous sufficiency
of the moment –
the automatic weapon on multiple lock –
electric plasmas
intransigent as angels.

Nothing is out of true:
purists whistle up
the bloodhounds,
those about to be executed
wear red blindfolds;

unhurried as lilies,
the disciples sit
at the holy supper
while the lovely boy
is hung *at a bough;*

no masking agent
for the heart
except insouciance –
the *mood indigo*
at the stroke of the green axe

willows breaking into F$^{\#}$ minor
for the flagellation
in a landscape,
the angel
at the inter-tidal funeral
announcing the end of time.

The Infinite Act

(after Stanley Spencer)

They are laying main drainage
in Cookham High Street;
the Queen's Swan-upper
nailed to the cross,
villagers craning
from the windows
like gazehounds at a tryst.

O the savour of Paradise –
as Adam names the animals
the leopards drop like honey
at their sweet difference;
stretcher–mules struggle
to rise for the resurrection
of the soldiers.

In the field hospital
dressings blush
into angelic orders,
forceps irradiate
the wound
the centre from which
all lines are drawen

What is charisma?
Love shirrs the petticoat,
the bride leans over
a chest of drawers,
Christ opens
the purple wardrobe
of his side.

But in the middle distance
Hilda has her foot
on the stile;
her husband's unanswered letters
stream past
terrible as a cloud
of witnesses;

the artist and his second wife
cannot perfect the error;
the disciples shoal

along the malthouse wall,
principalities and powers
smoke their bayonets,
Lord is it I, is it I?

Ave verum corpus
how do lovers know
one ecstasy from another
when they amaze
the moment
body to body
on the naked ground?

Thomas Traherne in the Orient

They shall look on Him whom they have pierced
clothed with the Southern Cross,
sun and moon on threaded rings
hurrying, tarrying

they shall hear
the blue cough of leopards
on feast days
in the bridegroom's chamber

they shall tongue
such syllables
the unicorn will kneel
to the Buddha

they shall see
young men
flex like angels
in the gem-mines

they shall sense
the seraphim
as elastic particles
rippling under haze

they shall dilate
like donors
before the sea-wind
in the cinnamon tree

they will be
such felicitous dust
in the balance
they will unsuppose

the body.

Gem-Dice from a Cinnamon Coast

I

The jetty is sprung
with split saplings,
the gourds warm-yellow,
the palm-tapper girdled
to the trunk.

Against the causeway
of crushed shell,
someone splits a coconut,
lets the milk
spill into the sand.

I no longer bleed each month;
but under the high salt tide
the barracuda run,
and downriver
village women prise open the oyster.

II

Natural to lie naked

Each act is different, you said,
the radiance of the body
barely begun

but I, glimpsing from the pillow
the moon lift
over the sill

the silted estuary beyond
where masted vessels
once thronged the river

knew the infinite act
to hold you in me
as I held you then.

III

We studied the night sky,
the gemmed axles,
the contained fires.

Easy, you said
to see Jupiter's second moon.

You gave me the glasses –
but how could I hold them steady
knowing at dawn
you would draw me out
like flame?

IV

It is over;
we drowse
as if purified;
the physicality
of miracle
to lie inward and naked;

but to contain
the urgency of innocence –
is there no lasting seal
when after ignition
hushed bodies
still burn?

V

How succinct the lovers –
they are pressed together like sweet kernels;
the warning bird calls all day long

under the hibiscus
they lie in their light trance
soundless as lizards

their kisses flicker,
mosque-swallows
blue-listing into the dusk

her breasts spice-islands
brushed
with vermilion.

If time is kept
it is by silken fuse
and trails of incense

the bee-eater
with liquid-yellow throat
strikes to remove the sting.

How succinct the lovers –
they draw from each other
that sweet extract which darkens with the season;
the warning bird calls all day long.

VI

The dark musicians
came over the night-sea
salt on the prow

they pressed their wild sweet stops
against the driving-silver
of the tide

the fire-eater
with throat thrown back,
smoke issuing above the surf;

such glancing accuracy
of flame along the flesh
I put my mouth to yours

and improvised.

VII

All day we waited
for the osprey
to stoop from the cross-mast,
clasp a burnished fish
in the flailing light

so how
between cinnamon coasts
could we have missed
that plunge
pounced with blood

a membrane over the eye
at the impact of entry?

VIII

Outside
with unseen accuracy
bats touch the skin of the water

inside – the smell of warm wax –
the urgent impress
of your body on mine

we are knit and reknit
like slow flares
in daylight

the moment timed
till it gives back
no altered echo

and upriver – the performing magic –
fire-throwers
exhaling the flame.

IX

The stilt-dancers
are blood-red
in the black night;
Orion overhead,
the young stars
burning hot and blue
the sand arena
blazing with cressets
and swirling, pleated silks;
the shaman
sliding gem-dice
under the lids

and beyond,
where the moon glitters
off the salt shrouds,
the lean, painted boats
swing from their moorings
on an inconstant tide.

FROM

THE WOUND-DRESSER'S DREAM

(1996)

Fidra's Song

(for David at Orinsay)

I

I hear a sound in the distance
hares in the open,
hawks digesting bone

an ivory scoop
clearing the breathing-hole
of the seal

oracles incised
with inscriptions
about rain

machines that tunnel
so silently, dice no longer
jump on a drumskin

the little gag of felt,
moonshine and lion
left to bury the dead.

II

The ear is pricked to
the sound of light itself

small flashing cymbals
as the sungod weeps bees

trumpets in the long moon
voces angelicae, flawless, waterworn

when the waves
are short singable lines

and the tongue moves by itself
Donne ch'avete intelletto d'amore

III

What is the look of the sound?

Any pressure on the black mosses
produces a kind of weeping

the moon beats its silk drum,
windows flex in the sea-wind

and the god of rainwater
lets lilies fall from his mouth.

IV

I saw three ships come
to the offshore isle

the lochan sullen with sky,
salt-lamb on the yellow wrack

the dead taking vehicles of enlightenment
over billowed vertebrae

thin strips of sheet-gold
ran down their cheeks

I couldn't bury her on a Sunday
but put a warm stone

into the vanishing cabinet
of the heart

and between fragrant rushes
the necessary beasts

bright with humility
graze the lazybeds.

Darwin in Patagonia

I brood on the process
of perfection and the less
perfectly gliding squirrels

in the parallel light of the afternoons
I study the creatures
constructed for twilight

I am never completely well;
the lakes hang like mica templates
in the brackish air

the winds pour from La Plata,
flies breed in the navels
of young mammals

I record the diving thrushes,
the woodpeckers
in the treeless wastes

the ice floes
which may formerly
have transported foxes;

across the straits
the barbarians multiply
The horse among the trumpets saith 'Aha!'

I take quinine and speculate
on the slashing claw
in the folded schists

but still dream
of Adam naming
the doubtful species

and wake shuddering
at the irreproachable design
of the eye.

The creatures preach to St Francis

They speak through my wounds
whether out of the body I cannot tell

the lion's eardrum flexing to the bees
in its own carcass

otters coupling in the burial boat

the stoat
who dances the questions put to him

reindeer sinews
lowering coffins through the ice

the mongoose tonguing the wind
from the feet of the dead

the muzzle of the snow-leopard
no more than after-image
in the extreme frost.

from Ruskin takes Rose La Touche to the Crystal Palace

I

How circumspect they are
under the cast iron,
their figures reduced
as in a *camera lucida*.

They do not touch
although fountains
solicit the humid air
and Amazonian lilies

carry cargoes
of quicksilver
to enhance
her pallor.

But he trembles
at her slight body
solarised against
the glazing-bars,

the sun behind
the quinine tree
swinging
its polished axe.

IV

As a boy on Chamonix
he had measured
the intensity of blue
with a cyanometer.

But what is the killing blue
that makes him kneel
suddenly on Skiddaw
and invoke the Litany,

her letter in his breast-pocket
between gold plates so thin
the snowline burns through them
purple and green?

By an unknown photographer

The lake is quite circular
and linen is left to bleach
under the salt bushes

the air full of unfired pigments –
the lightning man with axes
at elbow and foot

floating islands of peat
giving off a sweet savour
as they burn

but nothing ignites the trance
until the swans come in their thousands
and drink from the solid light

without breaking the seal.

Dancing the Mysteries

'I am the Word who did dance all things.'

Tinctura Sacra

Determined
to speak at the Synod
about sexual love between men,

and knowing death to be
the undisclosed miracle,
you postponed the operation for two weeks.

Three times in five years,
surgeons will expose the brain,
remove the tumour;

diminish sight and speech
with scalpels
of divining-silver.

But love is more
than its own likeness.
In the stern theatre

it is Cordelia
who plays the Fool.

Dancing the Mysteries is an elegy for a priest: Peter Elers of Thaxted, Essex. The Fourth Thaxted bell is known as 'The Dance Bell' and bears the inscription 'I ring for the General Dance', taken from an old Cornish carol, 'The Dancing Day'. Both this carol and the Morris dancers are traditionally associated with Thaxted.

Recasting the Bell
I ring for The General Dance

At the foundry,
men from the Morris Ring
gather for the casting.

The bell-mould bears
musicians, embossed dancers,
the hand of the Baptist.

They shield their eyes
against bright spillage
into cymbal, string and pipe.

Such emblems from the furnace –
the glowing throat of the bell
in the casting-pit,

the blaze in the clay;
and when the frieze of dancers
sheds its mould,

the rung-changes.

The Master Class

A consort are playing
Easter music at the hospice,
fantasias for viols.

Those who listen
are the benign
with aggressive tumours.

Notes fall like pencil-crystals:
lacrimae Christi
for the sickness unto death.

Is ripeness all,
when the dying are touched
by the inconsolable urgency of the flesh,

the rising thirst
intoned by the priest
on Good Friday?

The musicians bow
spiritual exercises,
suspensions, falling thirds;

silver-point studies
for a crucifixion,
Missa quinta toni.

Harmonics so tender
they might be intravenous,
tilt to the light;

and for a moment
bodies are no more
than counterweights of perspex

and listening blood
a fugue in red.

Dancing the Mysteries

I

*We'll come to the funeral
and how shall we dress?*

The Morris men
in waistcoats and white trousers
kneel at the altar-rail
after the elevation of the Host.

Breath and incense
cloud the chill air.

II

He has chosen his partner
from the dancing-ring;
Sing levy dew, sing levy dew.

The lissom boys
red satin wore
for Corpus Christi Day.

III

Outside the west door,
the Morris men dance
in the graveyard
with flowers in their hats.

But one –
the dancing-partner
playing the Fool,
in scarlet so red –

the white bloom
of his body,
the red stoup
of his blood –

ah dancer, ah sweet dancer

death
is the sun dancing.

Perfect Fifths

He wears
the purple sash of Lent
to the feast;
cannot drink
without slurping.

He, who was eloquent,
can no longer speak
of how the dove
hides
its illumined breast.

It is time for communion:
he cannot swallow
the wine;

is one of the wordless
who take the Word on their tongue.

But he listens
as we switch the tapes
at his bedside –
to the rising perfect fifths
for the raising of Lazarus.

Iron Stella
(for Gill)

Here, where once
we saw the vibration of cellos
rouse bats from the transepts,
there is only the great iron stella
between congregation and coffin.

'The rightness of the ritual,' you said;
a corona
for solder-lines on the skull;
bright salts from the furnace
for the office of the heart.

At the concerto,
spirits had flickered
between the stations of the cross –
the tinge of diastole
swept the white stone.

Strange visitation
in the deepening dusk:
to feel the pulse of music
after pall-weight,
the arteried bone,

the quickening
of the grafted thorn.

White Lent

Street-children
sing their garland
with backs to the dying

O Mary, O Mary
your true love is dead.
The robes they lay in fold.

The fair linen,
salt and candle,
burning-perfume of wounds.

Madonna of the goldfinch,
give us
tapers of chrism –

the lighting of lesions
is the game
in the rose-garden.

A Cherry-Tree Carol

With chalice and paten
by the bare spring tree,
tomorrow shall be my dancing day.

By the tower windmill –
its occasional creak against the sky –
tomorrow shall be my dancing day.

O lily-white boys
at the grave's dark lip
tomorrow shall be my dancing day.

The fantail spins,
the shining sails turn into the wind;
tomorrow shall be my dancing day.

'And having danced these things with us, Beloved, the Lord went forth. And we, as
though beside ourselves, or wakened out of deep sleep, fled each our several ways.'

A Christening by Snowlight

She had wanted you
christened between waters.

In the bridge-chapel
there was always
the intravenous lilt
of the river
flowing blackly below.

We stood in a light trance,
snow its own ceremony,
underglow of wax-myrtle
from the font
and as the priest tilted
the ewer,
the milk welling
like a hot tincture
inside her blouse.

Nightingales at Fingringhoe

How downbeat they looked
with their whitish breasts
in the underbrush

the estuary wearing
the moon at its throat,
the Queen Anne's Lace levitating,

a ship of blued-steel
drawn silently seaward
through the salt-marsh

as if it heard, beyond such song,
that other siren
of the young owls calling.

The Sleep Laboratory

We sleep lightly,
the moon irresolute
behind high fast cloud,
our rapid eye movements
monitored

precision instruments
for dreaming,
our temples wired
as the wild geese
fly over.

But nothing registers
the waking dream –
that glimpse of livid hellebore
in the unploughed square
under the pylon

Persephone
for the flower she once plucked.

After the bread-queue massacre

in Sarajevo,
Vedran Smailović puts on
white tie and tails
and plays Albinoni
among the ruins.

It is May –
blue with the outbreath
of swallows,
the gaze struck away
by the dazzle, the rubble

and at the edge of hearing
the sound for which
there is no music –
the dismembered
re-assembling their limbs.

The Wound-dresser's Dream

(In May 1819, John Keats considered signing on as a ship's surgeon.)

I

The sirens are those journeys
we never make,
compulsory territories
fabulous as blood,

the dog-star rising
over the cobalt mines,
shafts of flywheels
inflecting the engine-room.

What drums
on the sun's image
is the art
of the unlooked for,

swans dyed russet
by heavy metals,
wax figurines
under the embalming-wound,

that chance cargo
of boat people
in sacrificial dress
for the scenting of icebergs.

II

Do you not hear the sea?

I read *Lear* in the ship's pharmacy.
The crew pray
and clean their weapons,
birds rise like grapeshot
into the Egyptian blue,

the ship ghosting
the Sargasso,
only a mizzen raised
above the ambergris
and floating weed.

We sleep lightly
as falconers,
our cargo of quicksilver
soughing against
the sun,

no dew, no dew,
only incidental bleeding.
On the 6th.
the large white pig
executed on a curved ocean,

the baffled air
full of wild ginger,
the masts dropping
medicinal gums
into the sirocco.

Such investiture
of salt
I cough my proper blood
and digest nothing
but milk.

III

In the sail-maker's loft
we watched the great moon-moths
mate on the folded sails

compound insatiate ghosts
secreting syrups
against the glisten of salt.

Above, the shrouds belling,
and ashore, the sound of
heavy firing in the hills,

the wounded with their faces
covered in little squares
of mosquito-netting

IV

We anchor off the ice-plinth.
Is there no language
to localise pain?

We bleed the source,
sense the frazil-ice
through the hull

the scream of the ermine
frozen by its tongue
to the trapper's salt-lick

the sacred conversation
of sleighs shod with runners
of jawbone

the bluish foxes
that search
through a mountain of shoes

the silver-backed jackals.

V

In the room
off the Spanish steps
the tiny rattle
of salt through sea-lavender,
the sound of nuns
in habits blue as chicory
singing the sevenfold *Amen*.

Sweetwater rises
through the shingle,
the land-wind
green with pollen,
Xenophon's men still lying
honeyed
under the toxic rhododendron.

Heavy artillery
moves into the marsh samphires.
Without morphine
the medical orderly

at the battle of Grodek
cannot fit the look of wounds
into any imaginable world.

The white clinic falls silent
round the pure chromolithography
of a lung

In the wound-dresser's dream
the eyes of the beloved
are washed with milk.

Lindow Man

No words that I know of
will say what mosses are
yet we disturbed you
in the ancient sphagnum,
found mistletoe in your gut.

So what is unspeakable?
The sacred wound,
the triple death,
or simply sunlight
repeating such fiction?

Coleridge goes scuba-diving

How it intoxicates –
to have air for half an hour

the sea-bed
a quilt of India stuff
tasselled and fringed

a pillar of krill
passing through me
in *corpo transparente*

the flashing cipher
of eels as they graze
my wetsuit

glass-fish
with invisible viscera,
floaters in an eye

and even here
that other implausible cargo –
afterimage –

the swallow
supporting the sun
on one wing.

This Accomplishing of Light

(Florence, 1994)

I

You stood at the open window
dark with your own brilliance

and I, watching the light
touch nipple and lip
through the blown curtain

could think of nothing
but St Francis preaching
to the waterfall

and the running line of your breasts
between two waters.

II

I paint the light
that comes out of the body
as the glass flexes
and the Madonna conceives
through a slit
at the stomach
of her unbuttoned dress.

III

He has manifested himself
through the body

the burn of the moment
an iodide of silver

absolutely unalterable
in sunlight.

IV

What was in these bodies
that was so distinctly known?

Baroque violins
have a thread of metal
pressed into the gut.

Light whirrs;
the wind lifts gold leaf
with a squirrel's tail

the glitter on the string
like music.

V

It is noon; the bridge
rising over the river on mortar
made from egg-whites;

the lovers dovetail,
light passing through them
unabsorbed;

nor do they move
through time or space
any more than those magnets

hung in great telescopes
from spider's silk
that never twists.

VI

She stooping,
he with his head
against her belly,
the linen
wrapped round her thighs
like a mummy.

Which flows –
light or the body,
when the mirror
milks her skin,
and the sun through her lids
externalises the blood?

The anonymous Italian master
seeks the lightest tone
matizatura
for those signs
made on the body
and carried in the heart:

the disciple
with traces of gilding;
the angel isolate
against silk panels;
blood-sugars
of the golden bird.

VII *Fragment after Piero della Francesca*

Light fails

but not the process
of shining,

those wilder
less mimetic shores

where the dove
releases itself

from its white horizontal.

The Etching

I drew your body
directly on the plate,
slid the zinc
into warm acid –
brushed the bubbles
from the slight swell of your belly
with a feather.

Solvent and ghost –
as when we made love
like silkmoths
dissolving their own shroud,
outside, the men
laying cat's eyes,
and we unselved.

The Feather

(after Calvino)

*And when Jesus came
to the ruler's house
and saw the flute players
he said 'Depart,
for the girl is not dead
but sleeping'.*

Did he know
when he went in
and took her by the hand
that the hieroglyph
for the weighing of souls
was also the fundamental note
of the flute?

Seven thunders utter

and in the flash flood
ancestral carp
are flushed from the moat
of the imperial palace

pedestrians struggling up
from the subway
see them stream by
as if from a metal-foil machine

over the zebra crossing
through the traffic lights
past security camera
and the peril of mirrors

until far out
in the suburbs
where the afternoon light
is parallel to the sea

those taking
a remarkable view of bridges
hang over the cutwaters
and glimpse their gilded fins

still snagged
with the blue mosquito nets
and floating sleeves
of the concubines.

from Music for Kshantivada

I *Joseph Knecht Tunes the Clavichord*

It is the pure octave he is after –
he lowers his heartrate
like a marksman,
tunes the beating fourths and fifths
to his own pulse.

As master
of the glass bead game
he sets an equal temperament,
no longer hears
how *hazard has such accuracies.*

Suddenly
a billow of scent
through the open window,
soft-focus uprising
of elder in full flower

his heart outpacing
the fourths and fifths,
their impure intervals
flooding him
like an intoxicant

as if the property
of music
were not perfect tuning
but a disparity
that defines.

II *Glossolalia*

In the Japanese temple
the sprung floor
sings when anyone
steps on it

funeral jades
speak through
the nine orifices
of the body

and outside,
the nightingale
rinses the bubble
in its throat.

V *Varèse Improvises the Levitation of the Pyramids*

I require
the most coaxing acoustic –
the quartet
in one movement,
the zither with waxed silk strings.

I introduce
a siren, Chinese blocks,
hawkbells and ocarina,
ghost drum-set,
the roar of the desert lion.

They levitate
to tape alone,
rising *gradazione*
through the haze
by grace of electronics

and as they dream
at altitude,
flexing their photons
against the hot mouth
of the swallow

I build the echo

PARABLE ISLAND

(1999)

Footfalls

They came softly
into the underground chamber –
cave-divers
working by touch alone.

They found no red ochre,
no handprints,
only wolf-bones
and small footsteps in the mud.

Such clear heelmarks
showed the children
had been in no hurry
three thousand years earlier

but the divers never forgot
the racing
of their luminous watch-dials
as they heard

footfalls
(sole-sizes eight and eleven)
steal away
over the younger gravels.

Within North

A body on a sheet
of birchbark
in the acid peat,
an armband of foxfur,
vulpes vulpes
fluorescing bright green
in ultraviolet light.

The dead are masters
of diminishing return

but I still see her –
the dancer
with the antler head-dress,
binding her breasts
at the burial
of a stillborn child
to stop the milk rising.

Sourin

I

Read it simply:
the hawk as outbreath,
the sleeve of the wind
engraved with cloud-forms,
dusk unlatching its blues

and on the shingle
before the driftwood cross,
the priest lifting the word
against a fetch of shining water
as if the light had uttered.

II

The poetry is not firstly in the words;
a bright moon
holds shoals to the sea-bed

salt bruises the rose
to the vibration of a magical string
without sound.

III

How it glitters – the haul
between ebb and incoming

arctic terns fencing with mirrors
between the islands

the drowned pressing spindrift
to their faces
like little veronicas.

IV

The island makes its own cloud,
a soft drum-roll
kid-covered

a swan hangs
from the power-lines,
Odin realises the runes

and the imprint
of snow on water
says next to nothing.

Prima Nix

(for the nuns of Fetlar)

First snow
not yet dashed with a hare's foot.
We could go to our graves in white
not dead
but simply listening.

A simple interior,
the sound of the sea
through snowfall,
a cross-shaped cut in the membrane
behind the lens.

Prayer without words;
where the light meets the water
great areas left
unprinted
like a Japanese rice-paper painting.

Salt settles on the skin.
The ghostly disciples let
their heads fall forward
in the wind
like melancholy thistles.

Our Lady of the Isles
all the blues swallow one another.
Christ colours the quickbread.
The islands glide
into one body.

Blodeuwedd in Orkney

'And even now the owl is called Blodeuwedd.'

I have seen her hunt
at midsummer
when the night shines
as the day.

How can she
hide her face
in the glitter of salt
off the glass-green graves?

How can she hide
on white nights
the complicated reds
of the heart?

Eynhallow

Hartstongue,
an absence of squirrels,
the rip-tide glistening
like a single muscle

smallpox
and cabin-fever,
a merlin's eye
as the sun and moon

the insolence of zero –
in Christ's wounds
the sea-swallow
purchasing a nest.

Thomas Vaughan experiments with mercury

Always dangerous –
the water of the moon
in a mutable glass.

Was it vapour
or the heavy shining oxides
of yellow and red?

The pure *solutio*
when death came running
without feet

glass billowing
in the blast,
the birds outside

shaking metallic wings
as after rain.

St Brendan's birds

Not Sigurd's nuthatches
clattering in the brush,
but diamond vehicles,
their ribcages sprung with light
as they sing
the eight canonical hours

passerines,
weightless after migration –
magnetic particles
of iron oxide
in their retinas –
spirits fired with blood

as on St Kilda,
where if you put your ear
to the carbon-dating,
you hear the wrens
settle like small rain
on the tree-rings.

St Kilda

I weigh the heavy pollen count
against an ounce of indigo
as the trees vanish.

The islanders wear disposable shoes:
gannet-necks, slit from eye to breast,
feathered on the inside.

They salt-down the solan geese,
making their own blizzard,
guano giving a tincture to the sea.

In the blackhouses
there is the smell of silverweed, fulmar oil;
the babies have lockjaw

and from the end of the jetty,
eyes burning like millstones,
hark how the dogs do bark.

Lambholm

Here
at the salt edge of things,
the six-cornered snowflake
falls on simple moss.

Madonna of the Nissen huts –
your candles spit
before the creatures
of bread and wine

the sea reassembles its engines,
Italian prisoners of war
build the barriers
in a wolfish light

their prayers
tiny depressions
in the silence
like fossil raindrops.

Bleaklow

They nearly made it –
the thirteen men
in the Superfortress.

The engines still crouch there
like animals
of the four directions.

We came up from the Roman road,
saw the sun
graze the fuselage

heard the dead sough
through the cylinder heads
they probably never saw the ground

and we lay there
like lovers
the earth not moving.

Little Egypt

1 *Sandpeople*

These are the sandpeople –
fixed by fugitive stain
in the acidic soil;
rayographs
on light-sensitive ground,
the real become the sign.

When we divested them
they lay north-south
in pagan burial;
encaustic, exemplary,
preparatory drawings
in silverpoint;

their insufficiency of bone
fluorescing
under ultra-violet,
an amber inclusion
still hung
at the striation of the throat.

No excavation
catches the slenderness
of their chance melting;
taking the first cast
we remembered those
from Pompeii

but later
seeing the half-profile
in fibreglass,
felt only
bright sufficiency
outstripping the bone.

Little Egypt is a local name for Sutton Hoo, the Anglo-Saxon
burial-boat site in Suffolk, as well as a name sometimes given
to the Orkney island of Rousay, which has many early tombs.

2 *Tide-mill near Sutton Hoo*

It wasn't the pull of the tide I felt,
but the pull of men
raising the funeral-ship on the far shore;

how they hauled the clinker-built boat
over the red crag
up through the bracken;

sited it stern seawards
on the spur,
sank the gunwale below the barrow.

Such cold inlay –
only armourers on an enamel field
to fix the dye in the heart.

But then the tide turned, the sluice opened,
the medieval mill-wheels ground
as they had for the Black Canons

and looking out across the flood,
I remembered the inventory
of the sacrificial vessel:

bronze stag, stone sceptre,
baptismal silver
for the blood thickening inshore –

and I sensed how they crossed –
kingship,
the occurrence of mercy

and that bright error of judgement
which made the Saxon bird
flash through the lighted hall.

3 *Little Egypt*

Here in wartime,
army recruits packed
the excavated ship with bracken,
drove a glider trench
between the barrows

oblivious of
the tilt of the burial-boat
in the battle-ditch,
the king pillowed
amidship
between the tholes of the gunwale.

Weapons furnish sacrifice;
those who forged the rivets
for the ribbed hull,
left vizor and neck-guard,
sword and helmet,
cheekpieces of iron.

Now American planes
rise and fall
above the spur of the land,
whilst far below
where the estuary widens
the tide – gunmetal grey –
rises in the reeds.

4 *The Dig*

They map out the mound
like surgeons
dividing a belly,
scan for echoes.

Here the stern
of the burial-boat
was removed by ploughing.

On this female grave,
they uncover the goosewing
with which she swept out the oven;
the worn spiral
of an ammonite
where her dress
once opened at the breast.

It is quirkish of time
to leave only a purposeful echo
among the erratics:

this male body
buried in ploughing-position
beside his plough,
the eager figure
bent forward over the coulter –
fragile, passionate,
as if still reining-in
the light.

5 *Iken*

It was here
they broke the ground
for the burial of a stranger;

gave him
high above the estuary
a silent riding at anchor.

In the roofless nave
where the floor is shingle,
only baptism troubles the water;

on the chancel altar
a bleeding-bowl
of alluvial silver.

Nothing furnishes us
for such ebbs
of extraordinary fall –

for whether the miraculous
draught of fishes
is water or light

for the angel
figured on the luminous strand
with instruments of passion.

The bright source
of sacrament
is the dispossession of wounds;

how piercing-strange
the severity of the rite,
the inconsequence of the tide.

The Stowaways

They stayed on the ship for years,
never giving an identity.

For what was time
when they went for months
without seeing land or darkness

swinging in bleached hammocks
between counterweights
of sun and moon?

But in dream
seal-women gave them molluscs
as they disembarked

and when they woke
the luminescence persisted
on their hands and mouths.

Parable Island

Cold midsummer
and the middle of nowhere –
salt on flint,
the light behaving as it does
between islands.

In the old fever-hospital,
sage and juniper,
the surgeon's kit
and his divining-rods
laid in the grave.

Tinctures multiply.
When the sea-mist
burns off at noon,
you could slip a blade
between the sea and the sky.

Epiphany in Umbria

Driving between water and woodsmoke
I thought of St Francis:
how at a certain pitch, the sun
would strike both the stigmata
and the glass insulators
on the pylon.

Such melting abstracts –
all the while
the deer twinkling
their white underbellies
and looking like sunlight
before the sunlight hits them.

The Fallow Doe

It was she
who had caused the tail-back –
the rising vapour
not an overheated engine
but her breath
on the night air.

It still rives –
the way the exhaust
enhanced her aureole
as the engines idled,
she, heraldic in the headlights,
dying.

Burning the Vixen

How they run –
the red oxides
down the white mountain
as the villagers
burn her

smoke rising
through the balsam poplars,
her straw limbs
winnowing

and higher still
above the threshing-circle,
death the skier
leaving the snow
red behind him.

Tracking down the twelve-wired bird of Paradise
(after Alfred Wallace)

It took years,
the journey to the interior –
and then the bird
a little less than a thrush.

So vivid, he thought
for a moment
he must have glimpsed it
with the mind's eye.

Its flight across
the synapses
metallic green,
deep cinnabar

and before memory
altered it,

the scent of ginger flowers
rising so whitely

he could have wintered
in their throats.

Coleridge in Malta

His daemons brought fire-flies
through green solar spectacles,
young lobsters, hauled up dripping,
their claws lapis-lazuli
against the light.

When the ship was the ripple
he drank the mirage –
red and yellow camphor trees
walking by
with their little fevers

the sun dropping molten shapes
into the sea,
the momentum of imagining
a fragment of gold foil
in a glass vacuum.

Finding the right blue for the waterfall
(for Roger Warr)

Hiroshige knew –

so solid a blue
the Victorian tight-rope walker
could have crossed
in the declining sun
without her white pole gleaming.

It's a metaphysical act,
intensifying the blue –
swallows in slow-motion,
stars perched on the overfall
without trepidation

as when Orpheus played.

Herman Melville jumps ship

They say that blue
slows the passage of time –
so what was
the blue reflex
when I jumped ship
at the Marquesas?

How was it I could read
by the blue light
from the *noctilucae*
but not look up at the vanishing ship
or the natives running like grass
before the wind?

Reading the Light

This is seriously old light;
we read it, like snow

cattle moving from bright pasture
to bright pasture

the sea wearing the ship's wake
like a firing scar;

a certain luminosity,
a simple kill

the tear of the gazelle
borrowing the light

like one of those shakes
in music

performed by a tremble
of the finger.

Karumi

Early January,
snow falling without wind,
the hidden presence
of water beyond,
a white owl circling.

Any number of vanishing points:
capillary crystal,
high purity pounced with blood,
the spectral edge
between deepening and dispersal.

Slippage

It's a nice balance:
the climbers roped,
Himalayan ravens
rising from the valley.

When powder snow
leaves a vacuum
they are swept
into the zone

but never master
that other slippage –
curiosity
at riding the avalanche

while arresting ropes
burn to the bone.

Gyrfalcon

She came through sea-mist
trailing jesses,
her whiteness flecked
with ermine.

I waste nothing
of how she braced herself
against the space
between words

the light as linguist,
that syllable in the blood
when she turned
on a lazy axle

in the eye of the wind.

The Flight of Icarus

'What happens to the molecules is one thing: what happens in the onlooker is less calculable by far.'
FRANCIS SPUFFORD

How long did it last?
And is it still going on
for those who look up
from the lawn
with the kings and angels?

He is the sun's whipping-boy
flying into
the unseizable sign
which says
Deepen me.

Paint him
with raised brush-strokes
impasto −
all the big cats
kill with a neckbite.

And this particular body
this wax
that gives out a sound
if you tap it
with your knuckles

Look up −
unio mystica
where he catches the light
like a gilt shroud-pin
under the vapour trails

the gold hawk
with glass inlay,
etched on the zenith
like a clove
of Paradise.

As he suckles
he hears
the maternal heartbeat
in the background,
engine and ichor

the *duende*
of great sunlight
smoking the wax
until it runs
like anointing oil.

Which goldsmith
cast the sun
in a single piece
when he is fletched
with so many tongues

dropping seven skins
like a salamander,
as if he could
reassemble himself
before sundown?

in such a multitudinous falling
we expect sound
a winch to lower the angels,
the hiss of saltpetre
from undersea scars

the sky repeated
exactly in the water,
the sun's hawser
burning his hands
to the bone.

It fools the eye –
the discerning gesture –
the error on red
that makes an art
of bearing pain.

Pouring the sand mandala into the Thames

I still hear them —
the Buddhist monks
rasping their cones
of coloured sand

the mandala falling
in a fine stream,
the river wearing
its oiled silks.

It forces the flow —
the treachery of images —
the briar that blooms
as if unpremeditated

then bewilders the bone.

The Colony

How they run
from the island laboratory,
the albino rabbits.

The dew falls on their whiteness
as if they are filmed
with the moistness of the moon

zinc white, titanium white,
their breath hanging
on the salt air.

They graze right up to
the metal cradles
swilling with chlorine, phosgene

and then they breed,
whitely, whitely
under the crumbling cement

through each soft winter.

Potosí

The moon falls
like a metaphysician
on the silver city

so distressed a metal –
even the horses shod with silver
in the freezing streets

wagons, blue with graffiti
under the spoil-tips,
and at first light

mountain foxes,
red as cinnabar,
moving against the flow

between the silver-bearing lodes,
the upland snow.

Robert Louis Stevenson dreams of Orkney in Samoa

Last night
a wind came over the sea,
keen as a swan's bone,
particular with the dead.

I saw my father
and grandfather, inspecting
the major lighthouses
as the skerries smoked by.

Here, azure orchids burn,
kingfishers refract
the great white light –
but for a moment

I weigh the examined life,
the necessary exile,
against the way light behaves
between islands.

Salt over Skara Brae

(for Elizabeth Scarth)

I

It is not the sea-wind –
that salt in the eye
is sister and brother

under the heather
the dead are spring-heeled,
sand blown from the vertebrae

there is spruce on the shore
rafter of whale-rib,
bedding of blue clay

surf on the lintel
hazelnut shells,
elkskin and scapula

stones heat the water,
glistening lovers
run to red ochre

Queen of Peace –
put the salt-white host
on your tongue.

II

You brought stones patiently by boat
from midden and burnt mound;
volcanic stones,
quernstone and hollowed mortar,
stones from the recess in the scullery
which once housed the goose on her nest;
dropped them into the shallow loch
till the small island rose
and reflected meadowsweet
seeded the dusk.

Even now
from the high white drawing-room
I see you standing in freshwater
but looking seaward;

163

behind you, such shimmering replay,
I am not sure whether
the standing stones over the horizon
lean a moment into the wind,
or whether their shadows kneel
between waters.

III

Not unaccompanied burial –
under Scapa Flow
fish graze the guns
of the scuttled fleet,
the sea wears
the helicopter's circles
like a talismanic shirt;
below the swell,
heavy cups hang
in deepwater rows
from the ceiling of the serving room.

In the flare
above the blockship,
the *Hindenberg* lifts
from her bed
of compressed oil;
cormorants are runes on the rigging;
along the causeway
where the herring-shoals
once flashed,
fossil-fish mouth
from their several horizons.

How the whale-oil burns
with its wick of rush-pith;
and from the chapel
on Flotta,
the lit impulse
of the lost altar –
the tear-drop
shaped like a flame –
as if, above the open sea-hatches,
angels still freshen
with transcendence.

IV

This is the sung mass:
slingstones
for the songbirds of Quanterness

the white-tailed sea eagle
stripping flesh
before burial

a carved footprint
on the threshold
as rite for the limbless

the libation of the tribe
antler, young otter,
whole fish from inland water

a scattered necklace
where the freshly dead
sample exposure

how articulate –
the crimsoning ancestry,
the uneaten lamb in the tomb –

prisoners of war
bartering for meat
their model-ships of bone.

V

We were too late to take the causeway

but the hinterland is tidal,
the whole island in stormtime
washed by sea-water;

salt on the smelting-hearth,
silver cones
in a larch casket.

Our luminous hoard
the erosion of horizons
from low isles

to recover from the sandspit
the surgeon's lancet
the jaw of the porpoise

unset sapphires,
a spice-box of speckled jade –
against the incoming tide

a glimpse of the mainland.

VI

'*Sir John Franklin sailed from Stromness in 1845, seeking
the North West Passage, having watered at Login's Well.*'

No anchorage
eluded them –
only an alert from the crow's nest,
search-vessels
at the vanishing point.

The sledging party
have scurvy;
John Torrington wears
the blue wool
from the coffin lid.

The unmelting dead
still plot
their opaque passage
in the ship's library
under blankets of wolfskin;

but it flows through the permafrost –
their blue derangement –
the well
and the watering,
the imperfect lead solder.

VII

Such argosy –
the sunk merchantman
with cabins of sandalwood
in the brushed cobalt;
saltpetre and squirrel-pelt,
ivory gull and porcelain crab
on cannon under the kelp.

The sound is watered silk,
the sea foiled
by white sand
to simulate emerald;
that spume on the causeway
scrimshaw and crucible,
muslin from Bengal.

At no depth
are the drowned silenced.
Deliverance is watermarked;
a candle
of beachcomber's wax
still bleeds
for the maiden voyage.

VIII

> *'and on the thirteenth day of Christmas they travelled*
> *on foot over to Firth. During a snowstorm they took*
> *shelter in Maeshowe and there two of them went insane...'*
>   ORKNEYINGA SAGA

Mercy is unseasonable –
pilgrims glimmer
through the sleet,
the skull
a bone lantern.

The delirious
glimpse longships
in the blizzard,
the winter king and queen
departing for the hunt.

Blue virgin –
those who go to Byzantium
take no treasure
redder
then Pentecost.

Holiness hones –
over Jerusalem
slim blades
crimsoning
the solstice.

Red Christ
in the white mound –
this is the surgery
of light
they came unto the sepulchre
at the rising of the sun.

IX

We made such calm departures –
salt on the causeway,
rigging bleached by the wind;
jellyfish gliding past
like lampshades under the swell.

We did not ask
if sun or cymbal
burnished the silence,
cloudscape or coastline
receded with the seal singing;

and as for inland music –
we remembered none
except the rustling field
of the cloth of gold where
the warrior is buried with glass bowls.

But with hindsight,
we should have seen by the light
through the flint arrowhead,
borne dangerous cargoes,
burned to the waterline.

A LITANY OF HIGH WATERS

(2003)

Scarecrow

There's a man in the corn

Rest easy my dear

With red on his hands

Poppies my dear

He's crowned with storm-birds

Quickthorn my dear

I saw his face in the lightning's fork

Sockets clear my dear

The driven rain was the world's wide tear

Just so my dear

If I laid my eyes in, would you take him down?

O no my dear

Girl on Silbury Hill
(for Graham Arnold)

You would think her
cool as a flute
from the long-bone of a swan,
her flesh the lit wax
for all suppressed pallors

until the tributaries
of the Kennet rise
through the chalk
and the reflected landscape
inverts
the white of her breast.

Joseph of Arimathea crosses the Somerset Levels

He could have made it by boat
from Bristol to Glastonbury
over the flooded withy-beds

only a smell of sapwood,
bright yellow wolf-moss,
rotten willows shining through the gloom

osiers wearing mirrorwork
after rain, then that other
feast of lights

the sullen thorn
flowering suddenly,
its stem still sealed with wax.

Holy Thursday

It took ages
washing the disciples' feet –
the passers-by incurious,
vapours rising from vents
in the sidewalk.

Such crazy intimacy –
a bowl of water,
fire-washed linen,
snow shovelled in piles
amid the graffiti.

What kind of sanction was this –
the unbidden hands,
the laving of the feet,
and he, kneeling,
his incidental powers
theoretical as light?

Walking the tide-line on Ash Wednesday

Marginalia –
waters rewriting the landscape,
the wrack a deep fox-colour

velvet crabs in the eel-grass,
the sun slipping
its golden burnous

graveyards
shutting up the sea
with doors

a daylight moon
placing ashes
in a silver vessel

the lesser litany
of salt on shingle,
and further out

effleurage,
the hare's fur effect on glaze,
a killing in water.

The Boarding Party

It spooked us –
the boat ghosting
the Sargasso

his shorn hair
and snatches from the *Messiah*
on the cabin floor

a copy of Einstein
where he'd sat naked
with a soldering iron

the life-raft
lashed on deck,
the safety-line unhooked

My reflexes amaze me.
They're so fast you know
I catch things almost before
they start falling

The nightingale's not telling

The Qingzhou buddhas
are laid
torso upon torso
in the burial-pit

their limestone sleeves
full of fossil-pollen
as if to leaven
any long fallow

the fabled glow
from their bodies
inscrutable
to the last.

The Hangar Ghosts

They come
as the hare dozes
in the dustless air

desultory
in their flying helmets
between huge drums of straw

silent, allspeaking
against the bruiseless blue,
as if the fuselage

still judders through
their bone-marrow
between sorties

and the sky,
serious with snow,
closes behind them.

The Amber Room

You can feel it –
the deep patience
of the amber room –
all those carved panels
shipped from the cellars
of Konigsberg
and stashed underground.

Resins
from the first forests,
glowing, oversnowed,
the sprung-release
of their slow fires
indexing the dark

as when the explorer Kane
put cunning mirrors
in the cabins
of his dying men
until the black hold
burned
with pollens laid down
under a midnight sun.

Eclipse at Skara Brae

There it was –
reflected in the roof
over the Neolithic village,
bloom of salt
on the glass
like a grave-mirror
misting at the breath.

And the dead?
Did they pluck
the daylight-altering herb
during those moments
of lovely dislocation,
and feel time
supple

as one of those
sword-blades
which can be bent back
until the point
almost touches the hilt,
before springing back
undistorted?

Tundra

It is dead quiet over Siberia.
For three days
there has been nothing to see
from the Graf Zeppelin
through the cloud.

In the silken interior,
a priest reads the lesson:
Jonah, praying
even out of the fish's belly
while the Northern Lights
crackle and swish
against the ship's fabric.

These things happen –
the fixed harness of the stars,
a spare parachute
for the stowaway,
chance ignition.

Landscape with five-barred gate

They are like two orchestras
playing at different pitch,
the act and the art
of remembering.

Not so much the land
as what you make of it –
the gate opening both ways,
the larks unlocated

and sheep–shearers
rolling warm fleeces against
the slowness of the waterfall
in the distance.

The Reversible Waterfall

I still hear it –
the sound of the heart ceasing

your hands turning blue
as if redressing the light

while outside,
like perfect disciples

the migrating birds
go back on themselves.

Since then, I dream
of a reversible waterfall

the river rushing over the rocks
at low tide

then the sea rising
to replenish the river

the creature of water
clouding, clouding

like this flux of the eyes,
this faculty of weeping.

The White Shell

(for my mother)

No headstone –
just your ashes
scattered on white flowers
for the dead take up
too much inconsolable space.

Candour was your quality,
as in that Japanese print
where the shell is unseen
but everything whitens
with its referred radiance

the way snow accumulates silence.

Garter Snakes Drinking from Snow

They pour
from the naked rock
thirsting, innumerable,
while every surface smokes
in the sudden sun.

Simply the one thing –
a long luminous draught
as they swallow
the snow like immortals,
before mating.

The Loneliness in the Garden

Roses –
their cold reds
falling unbruised
through the black hours.

Nothing simplifies
like moonlight:
great wedges of shade
on the lead-white lawn

and several birds
in the tree of life,
sure-footed,
travelling nowhere.

Rimbaud and the ship from Aphinar

Here in Marseilles
there are shipping lines everywhere
but I can't find a single one
for the enchantments
sitting on my brain.

I would trade in a cache
of elephant tusks
for a passage back
to the African sun.

In Abyssinia
I sold scissors,
aromatic gums, obsolete rifles –
each ounce of indigo
blistered past.

As a deserter
on St.Helena,
mildew fell like salt-frost
on my skin.

In my self-portaits
I aimed to give not just
the hush of disguise,
but the strongest impression
of there being no-one there.

So it will come
unlooked for
out of the vivid haze,
the ship from Aphinar
to Suez.

I am paralysed
and will embark in good time.
Let me know
when I can be carried aboard.

Dreaming of the Dogger Bank

This was no dreaming act –

the waves came in
like grey wolves
without breaking stride,
over willow fish-traps,
through the fowler's nets.

Does the sea recall
how it lifted our ancestors
from their pastoral
at that last high-tide
of the known world?

Even now
when the waters reconsider,
you can sense deer
outpacing the shoals
through the driftwood of Dogger

and glimpse far down
the dripping rime,
the altered time,
owl and hare
in habits of bright dew.

Finisterre

What's in a name?
The end of the earth,
sea-eagles in passage
from nowhere to nowhere.

We have lost
the infernal blue
of those shipping lines
to elsewhere.

Not even the cargoes
of ice and amber,
opium and camphor
still hanging in there.

The magnetic horizon,
those arteries of otherness
gone – as though
they never were.

Landfall

(after Cavafy)

We have seen everything –
clouded leopards,
speckled ox and delicate owl,
revolution
in imperial orchards

the oil-slick of ships
lying in quarantine
under the volcano,
the bright green bones
of the garfish

water silkworms,
that last stitch
in a sailor's shroud
through gristle
between the nostrils

turquoise from Sinai,
vermilion, turmeric,
indigo-merchants
in their summer kiosks,
the grafting of the golden peach.

We travelled lighter
than the purple heron
leaving its footprint
on the steps
of the Buddha.

How can we keep
the beautiful error
of never having arrived,
when winds blow
through the gantries

from the Great Divide?

A LITANY OF HIGH WATERS

Falcon on a blue field

1

We seek *falcones gentiles*,
great northern gerfalcons.

Everywhere, the colour of exile –
silica, sulphur

arctic foxes in their mottled summer blue,
ashes white unto harvest.

In the unspeakable interior
the rivers drop like axes.

Our old frostbite re-opened
through the white nights

so we sang
from the sagas

'We are snowed on with snow
and smitten by rain
and drenched with dew.
We have long been dead.'

Only then, did the falcons
fall out of the middle air.

2

You lure me
as if flesh
were the only
magic accessory

the heart
a parcel of silks
dying and rising
in red.

But seeing the marrow
of wingbones
laid on
a white gauntlet

I wonder if it is
the making
or unmaking
of the heart

whistles me down.

Christ in the lava fields

This is the white night
of the soul –
frost and lichen,
obsidian,
the nine natures of the raven,
and grass nowhere.

Solitude outside geography
or in it. No matter.
For these are
the spiritual meadows
where the lava will kneel
before the Fire Sermon.

Sea-swallows

Truly birds of appetite,
wearing their long habit of light
with vehemence

following the midnight sun
from pole to pole
as if absolving the dark.

Surely they were there
before anything was,
unsung and beyond metaphor?

The knowledge of water

After nine thousand years
a Chinese flute
made from the wingbone
of a red-crowned crane
is blown again.

Memory has no perfect pitch

but for a moment
the air holds
the flight of birds
out of deep time
the way water
remembers an eclipse.

The Ballad of Ruby Tuesday

Its the same here –
stink of stockfish everywhere –
North End, Fisher's End,
Pilot St, St Ann's St.
Nothing but sedge and samphire
under a threequarter sky.

On nights
when moonlight washes
through True's Yard,
I take out my shoes of catfish
and walk the blue wharves
with their bales of Lincoln scarlet

squirrel-skins, sturgeon and beeswax,
linen and eels,
and tell the salt-panners
how my mother
steamed dark sweet ryebread
over the cooling lava.

Like the green girl,
I shall marry a merchant
of Iceland in Lynn.
On that night
Brother Wolf,
swallow the moon.

The Last Sorcerer

What do I hear
when I stalk local fevers
in the shape of a fox?

Willow, lowgrowing
over pillow-lava,
the purchase of lupin on pumice

a winter wren
in the hinterland
orgasm of young corn along the coast

ripples
where the Hidden People pass
in their fishing boat

undermusic –
quillpens on calfskin,
a raven predicting the weather

padding of reindeer
before grindstones
close behind them

cattle keeling over
as they graze
the sulphurous grass

Thor pulling on his iron gloves
while the sap moss
opens in silence

Litanies

Moonlight floods
Saturday market place
and floats St Margaret's
like the sun at highwater

Highwater   1st March 1949
Highwater   11th March 1883
Highwater   20th March 1961
Highwater   31st January 1953
Highwater   11th January 1978

In Hallsgrímkirkja
the light off the stone
whitens with
the Great Winters

The Great Glacier Winter   1233
The Great Snow Winter   1405
The Little Ice Age
The Later Plague   1494-1495
The Winter the Horses died   1313

*In 1445 three Lynn men left the port for Iceland
in a dogger called the Trinity*

We see northern lights
through closed lids,
the ice in our eye.

It is never dark.
The moon from her eccentric window
cries New Moon, No Moon.

The Virgin holds a lens
of fire and dew, but our hearts
have shrunk with the cold.

Maris stella – guard our cargo
of silver buttons and knives
on the blue shingle.

Sew us into our hammocks
with seal-wives,
like the dead.

When autumn packs
our bodies with salt
we will return

and lay on the eelgrass
scrimshaw, sulphur,
and the precious white bellies

of ermine

The ambivalence of islands

I am here
after waiting in strange airports,
all time's succulence
for the taking.

Fabled mammals,
striped marlins,
a balsam cargo smouldering
on the horizon

the gypsum towers
of Atlantis
melting like sugar
in the rain.

The Thirteen Days of Christmas

On the first day of Christmas
a red rose is offered for the rent of Castle Rising

On the second day of Christmas
priests cast salt on the water in the shape of a cross

On the third day of Christmas
phalaropes walk in circles on the river-bed

On the fourth day of Christmas
the sagacity of beasts rises like vapour
through the turf houses

On the fifth day of Christmas
Christ sleeps on the pillow lava

On the sixth day of Christmas
six gentle falcons fall out of the sun

On the seventh day of Christmas
reindeer kneel in the interior

On the eighth day of Christmas
blubber lamps bob along Blubber Creek
to St Margaret's church

On the ninth day of Christmas
angelica leaves its signature in the fiery liquor

On the tenth day of Christmas
the best quill is taken from a swan's left wing

On the eleventh day of Christmas
eleven trolls are struck by sunlight
and turned to stone

On the twelfth day of Christmas
Mount Hekla lifts her cloud of unknowing

On the thirteenth day of Christmas
the last great auk comes up out of the sea,
flightless in the unforgiving light.

Notes

Falcon on a blue field (184)

King Haakon of Norway, writing to Henry III about a present of great northern gerfalcons that he was despatching to him, said *his falconers had been two whole years in Iceland seeking them, enduring unbelievable cold and hunger.* On the medieval King John cup in the Guildhall in Lynn, such falcons are vividly portrayed. I am indebted to Ursula Dronke's translation of *Baldrs draumar*.

Christ in the lava fields (185)

On July 20th 1783, with the lava from the Laki eruption only a little over a mile from the church at Kirkjubaejarklaustur, Jón Steingrímsson preached his Fire Sermon. As he preached the lava stopped flowing. The quotation about solitude is taken from the *Journals* of Thomas Merton.

Sea-swallows (185)

The sea-swallow is the Arctic tern, *Sterna paradisaea*. It summers in the Arctic and winters in the Antarctic, always following the light.

The knowledge of water (186)

Water is sensitive to very slight changes in electrical and magnetic fields and records the dwindling of light during eclipse.

The Ballad of Ruby Tuesday (186)

Icelandic children were reputedly kidnapped 'especially by men from Lynn and Newcastle' during the 15th century. In one version of the Green Children legend, the girl survives and marries a man from King's Lynn.

The Last Sorcerer (187)

The last sorcerer, Thórdur Halldórsson, is believed to live under Snaefell-sjökull, the Snow Mountain Glacier, which can be seen from Reykjavík.

In 1445 three Lynn men left port... (188)

The inspiriting of this poem came from Dorothy Owen's *The Making of King's Lynn*.

The ambivalence of islands (189)

Although this poem has an exotic touch, it sprang from my glimpsing Surtsey, one of the volcanic Westmann Islands, which arose miraculously from the sea between 1963 and 1966.

The Thirteen Days of Christmas (189)

In Iceland, Christmas Day is added to the traditional twelve days of Christmas. Mount Hekla, a volcano not far from Reykjavík, is often shrouded in vapour. The great auk's last major breeding ground was on Geirfuglasker, an island off southern Iceland.